Justice: redressing the balance

THE LEGAL ACTION GROUP (LAG) is a charity founded in 1972. Its purpose is to promote equal access to justice for all those members of society who are socially, economically or otherwise disadvantaged. To this end, it seeks to provide support to the practice of lawyers and advisers; inspire developments in that practice; campaign and promote improvements to the law and administration of justice on behalf of disadvantaged people; and stimulate debate on how services should be delivered. It publishes a range of law books, a monthly journal, *Legal Action*, runs a programme of continuing professional development courses and promotes policy debate.

Further information can be obtained by contacting the Legal Action Group, 242 Pentonville Road, London N1 9UN, UK; telephone (+44) 171 833 2931; fax (+44) 171 837 6094; e-mail: lag@lag.org.uk; DX 130400 London (Pentonville Road).

ROGER SMITH has been director of the Legal Action Group since 1986. He is a solicitor and honorary professor at Kent Law School.

Justice: redressing the balance

Roger Smith

Legal Action Group
1997

This edition published in Great Britain 1997
by LAG Education and Service Trust Limited
242 Pentonville Road, London N1 9UN

British Library Cataloguing in Publication Data
A CIP catalogue record for this book is available from the British Library

ISBN 0 905099 78 8

Typeset by RefineCatch Ltd, Bungay, Suffolk
Printed in Great Britain by Bell & Bain Ltd, Glasgow

Contents

List of tables

Preface

Legal aid in England and Wales is at a crossroads. This book has been published at a particularly important moment, a few months after the election of a new Labour government. A review of legal aid and civil justice, conducted at the behest of the government by Sir Peter Middleton, will be completed at around the same time. The constraints of government planning probably mean that key decisions will be made very soon after its publication.

The book, by and large, represents the policy of the Legal Action Group (LAG). The necessary speed of production means, however, that it has not proceeded formally through the approval process that, for example, was possible for its predecessor, *A Strategy for Justice: publicly funded legal services for the 1990s*, which was published after the 1992 election. As a result, its personal authorship has been acknowledged and not collectivised. Its chapters on policy represent a collection of ideas very much within the spirit of LAG's approach but their detail remains formally unapproved and could yet be disowned. This is less of a problem than it might be since the fundamental objective of this publication is to broaden debate rather than to advocate any particular masterplan.

The contribution of LAG's committee should be acknowledged as the book's form has been adapted over the last nine months to changing political circumstance. So too should that of all the staff at LAG.

The book is being published as part of LAG's 25th anniversary celebrations and its promotion has been greatly assisted by the funds provided by a group of sponsors to whom we express our thanks. Another element of the 25th year activity is the launch of a new membership scheme. Details of this and other LAG activities can be obtained from LAG at the address on page ii.

Roger Smith, Director
Legal Action Group
London, UK

CHAPTER 1

Access to justice: a principled approach

> The civil justice system in this country urgently needs reform. The time is right for change. The public and businesses want change, and the majority of the legal profession.
>
> Lord Woolf *Access to Justice: Final Report* (1996), para 21.

> Most people now feel that the legal system does not work for them. The vast majority of people on middle or low incomes are effectively denied access to justice.
>
> Labour *Access to Justice: Labour's proposals for reforming the civil justice system* (1995), p1.

Clarion calls for reform of our justice system echo down the decades. Every so often, there is significant movement. In the 1870s, after long debate, the civil courts were reorganised along something like their current lines. In the late 1940s, legal aid legislation was introduced in an attempt to recognise the law's democratic deficit, the exclusion of the poor. The reforms to be expected of the remainder of the 1990s are, as yet, unclear. Nevertheless, it may not be too fanciful to suggest that policies on access to justice, at least in relation to the civil matters which are the focus of this book, are at a crossroads. Decisions to be made in the next five years, the lifetime of the current parliament, will form a new approach dictated by the dual, and largely conflicting, pressures of extending democratic access to all society's institutions to all its members and the restraining of state expenditure.

The first quotation above comes from Lord Woolf's report on civil justice, the final version of which was published in 1996. The fate of his proposals – for greater control of cases, more standardisation of procedure, fast-tracks and multi-tracks – hangs in the balance. The second comes from the Labour Party document on its legal services policy passed at its 1995 conference. It called for the transformation of legal aid into a community legal service. Swept into office by an unexpectedly massive majority, Labour's new administration, led in relation to these matters by Lord Chancellor Lord Irvine of Lairg QC, announced an immediate and short-term review of legal aid and civil justice. This decision was no surprise and complied with a promise given before the election. The identity of the reviewer was. Lord Irvine, allegedly rebuffed by at least one business figure, chose Sir Peter Middleton, former permanent secretary of the Treasury and current chairman of Barclays Bank.

The weight to be given to this review is uncertain. It is planned to last barely 100 days. This cannot be time enough to deal fully with the problems facing those who are poor and unlucky enough to face the need to go to law in the civil courts. The best that can be hoped is that Sir Peter Middleton will set a course for the future development of more detailed policy. This book, to be published contemporaneously with Sir Peter's interim report, is designed to encourage debate on the political options facing the new administration. In relation to legal aid and civil justice, Labour starts with no clean sheet. Much has been written under its predecessor administration that cannot be unwrit and which will unavoidably dominate future developments. The Conservative Lord Chancellor, Lord Mackay, established – and backed – Lord Woolf on his crusade for a simpler justice system. He also developed, over a number of years, an approach to drastic reform of legal aid that would have involved the introduction of a cap to its cost and what in effect would have been compulsory competitive tendering for its practitioners. The Legal Aid Board, charged with the administration of legal aid in all courts except the highest criminal ones, has also invested years in developing its plans for reform. In these circumstances, the ship of state has all the manoeuvrability of a supertanker under full steam.

One option no longer available is to wait, see and do nothing. The late 1990s must be a time of change because the pressures of current arrangements are no longer containable. Access to justice is not at an acceptable level; too many people are excluded. This might by itself not be enough to precipitate reform. More pressing for any government, however, is the question of cost. The cost of justice is a deterrent to individuals who are funding their own litigation. It is a burden for the state to extend its subsidy out of public funds. Governments in all democratic societies feel a common pressure on their finances. The democratic impetus that has driven constitutional advance over the last century and more, in which the institutions of the state have been

opened up to once-excluded groups, now suffers check, in this country as elsewhere. Governments around the developed world are growing more reluctant to ask their more prosperous citizens to pay the
price for full social emancipation of the poor.

This book is a contribution to the debate on social exclusion
renewed by the election of Labour after 18 years in political exile. It is
oriented around Labour's one extended statement of policy, published in 1995, albeit that the status of this document is unclear. It was
largely the work of a shadow spokesperson on legal affairs, Paul
Boateng MP, who was posted to another ministry after the election.
However, reference to the document has been used to give form to
arguments which are not, in their essence, party political. The policies
advocated herein are much the same as those presented to the Conservative government in 1992 and published by the Legal Action
Group as *A Strategy for Justice*. The case for access to justice can be
made in a variety of different languages. The orientation of the book
is designed to show a Labour administration how it could increase
access to justice; restrain public expenditure and implement its pre-
election legal strategy. The battle for greater rights to the disadvantaged is, however, to be waged on a number of different fronts, with
correspondingly varied rhetoric. Below are two judicial quotations on
the same ground:

> Access to the courts is a constitutional right; it can only be denied by the
> government if it persuades Parliament to pass legislation which specific-
> ally – in effect by express provision – permits the executive to turn people
> away from the court door.[1]

> The Court has . . . recognised a narrow category of civil cases in which
> the State must provide access to its judicial processes without regard to a
> party's ability to pay court fees.[2]

They are from judgments, made within three months of each other at
the end of 1996 and the beginning of 1997. The first was penned by
Mr Justice Laws, of the High Court in London, and the second by the
justices of the US Supreme Court in Washington. They imply positions
which are, fundamentally those espoused by this book. First, access to
the courts, and more broadly to justice, is a constitutional right which
the government should, in principle, actively make a reality for those
for whom poverty or other disadvantage would otherwise be a barrier.
Second, access to justice requires policies that go beyond legal aid and
the provision of lawyers or advisers: all barriers to justice must be
considered and minimised. Thus, a Mississippi mother was given the
transcript of the judgment which she needed to challenge a custodial

order in relation to her two children even though she could not afford the usual $2,000 fee. In this country, Mr Witham, unemployed and in receipt of income support, was permitted to begin his libel case, even though he could not afford a newly introduced £500 fee.

Access to justice: ten principles

There is remarkably little consideration of the first principles that should underlie policy on the justice system. In default, policy-making by the Lord Chancellor's Department (LCD) tends to appear dominated by the task of setting and meeting its spending estimates. Any coherent approach to policy-making should begin from statements of first principle before extending to the pragmatic. The following are ten propositions that underlie the argument of this book. Any alternative programme of reform should similarly reveal the principles upon which it advances its case.

1. Access to justice is the constitutional right of each citizen.
The words of King John's declaration to his barons in Magna Carta, though needing a little updating in relation to gender, record something as close to a constitutional principle as our jurisdiction can aspire: 'To no man will we sell, to no man will we deny or delay, right or justice.' Denial of legal advice, representation or of access to adjudication can all amount, in circumstances such as those encountered by Mr Witham, to a denial of justice. Raising court fees to the extent that Lord Mackay intended could also be construed almost as an attempt to sell it.

2. The interests of the citizen should predominate in policies on access to justice and not the interests of the providers of services.
This should be self-evident but the next chapter traces how the legal aid scheme was established by, and has consistently reflected, the interests of the lawyers who provided services and were paid for doing so. The results have been by no means all negative. England and Wales probably has as fine a system of criminal legal aid as can be found anywhere in the world. Nevertheless, in a time of financial restraint, we have to recognise the ultimate purpose of the justice system. Special interests, even those as entrenched as, say, the Bar, should not be allowed to overcome the fundamental purpose of expenditure.

3. The goal is not only procedural justice but substantive justice.
In the formulation espoused by Lord Woolf, the civil justice system must be 'just in the results it delivers'[3] as well as in its procedures. Defendants in the show trials of Nazi Germany and the Stalinist USSR had lawyers: procedures may be scrupulously legal and yet substantively unfair.

4. People have need for legal assistance both in relation to civil and criminal law.
Civil justice is often seen as having different and, in some ways, inferior claims to criminal justice. A number of foreign jurisdictions provide much more effective legal aid for criminal cases than for civil ones. Scotland spends close to three-quarters of its legal aid budget on crime. Some Australian jurisdictions have suspended eligibility for civil cases at times of budgetary crisis. Legal aid spending is much more balanced in England and Wales but subject to the danger of going in the same direction as spending becomes more contained. Overall, civil justice, particularly when family work is excluded, tends to be regarded as the law's poor relation, as Lord Woolf lamented in his interim report:

> The growth of criminal and family business has meant that their demands have tended to prevail over those of civil business, to the disadvantage of the latter.[4]

5. Access to justice requires policies which deploy every possible means towards attaining their goal including reform of substantive law, procedure, education, information and legal services.
Compartmentalised thinking and departmental boundaries make this otherwise reasonable statement particularly difficult to implement. Broadening the approach will require new dimensions to the role of the Lord Chancellor's Department and the Legal Aid Board.

6. Policies on legal services need to deploy a 'portfolio' approach of a wide range of provision, some publicly funded and some not, some provided by lawyers and some not.
Integration of approach is a key concept to be applied to every aspect of how access to justice may be attained. We need to consider the full range of ways in which the citizen may receive assistance with the law.

7. Programmes of reform must take account of the realistic levels of resources but these should be seen as limiting policies rather than defining them.
Concentration on limiting cost must not exclude consideration of the fundamental purpose of the expenditure. Limited resources must be regarded as a restriction on the means not ends of policy.

8. Within civil law, more attention should be given than previously to the particular legal needs of poor people currently excluded from legal aid.
The scope and eligibility of legal aid has reduced so much that simple extension of the *status quo* is not acceptable. Legal aid is not effective enough in its present state: too many are ineligible for assistance yet manifestly unable to fund their advice or representation.

9. The full potential of technological advances must be harnessed.
Developments in information technology may make cheaper services possible, though considerable care is needed to preserve effectiveness. New technology offers the promise of extending services to those who do not currently receive them.

10. The constitutional right to be regarded as innocent until proved guilty should be respected as a cardinal principle of criminal law.
This book concentrates on civil justice because it reflects the topical issue of concern in the legal aid debate. In the light of various proposed reforms of the criminal justice system, however, it appears apposite to restate among this list of first principles a commitment to the basic principle that must underlie the state's approach to law and order.

Accessible justice and social exclusion

Policies on access to justice, like those relating to anything else, must relate to the characteristics of the society in which they operate. Our society is very different from that of 50 years ago when legal aid was first implemented as part of the welfare state. Three groups are emerging: those who are very comfortably well off on almost every relevant index such as job security and income, home tenure, savings, etc; those so poor that they are increasingly identified as an 'underclass' excluded from many aspects of society; and those in between, marginal groups on the edge of poverty and full of insecurity. The precise dimensions of these groups is open to debate. One critic, *Observer* editor Will Hutton, convincingly argues for the perception of what he calls a 'thirty, thirty, forty society':

> ... the first 30 per cent are the *disadvantaged* ... the second 30 per cent are the *marginalised* and the *insecure* ... The last category is the *privileged*.[5]

These figures relate to legal aid because the eligibility for green form legal advice is around the first 30 per cent figure and that for civil legal aid not far behind (see p23), ie, legal aid and advice is available for the disadvantaged group but not for many of those who might be seen as marginal. What is more, the state of the disadvantaged has worsened in recent years: they are now considerably more needy than in the 1950s. The pattern of poverty is changing, increasingly centred on children. On the Child Poverty Action Group's calculation, a third of all children (4.3m) live in poverty (defined as 50 per cent of average income after housing costs). In 1979, the comparable figures were 1.4m and 10 per cent.

Poverty can be variously defined but an incontrovertible bottom line is income support, the basic income replacement means-tested benefit. As many as 14m people are eligible for this each week (around a quarter of the population). An even more disturbing statistic is that eight per cent of the total population – 4.7m of the 14m identified above – live below income support levels, because of their failure to take up benefits to which they are entitled.[6] This figure has particular importance because it means that receipt of income support cannot safely be taken as a 'passport benefit' which identifies and defines the poor. Lord Mackay acceded to a general government policy of pass-ported eligibility for services by reference to basic means-tested bene-fits. However, a well established problem of means-tested benefits with low eligibility is the creation of a poverty trap whereby every pound earned above a certain figure can lead to reduction in benefits of a greater amount (see p75). For those caught at particular levels of low income, legal aid contributions can combine with other reduc-tions in any additional income to take them below the government-accepted minimum level of income, creating a very real justice element to the wider phenomenon of the broader poverty trap.

In the 1980s and early 1990s, England and Wales rapidly became more and more unequal. To quote the Child Poverty Action Group:

> In the last decade and a half, the living standards of the poor and affluent have been moving in opposite directions – a fall for the poorest and huge rises for the richest ... between 1979 and 1992/93 the poorest tenth of

the population . . . experienced a fall in their real income of 18 per cent after housing costs, compared to a rise of 37 per cent for the whole of society and a staggering leap of 61 per cent for the top tenth.[7]

The effect was recognised even by Kenneth Clarke as Conservative Chancellor of the Exchequer who saw:

> . . . the growth of a so-called underclass as the most formidable challenge to a secure and civilised way of life throughout the developed world. Our society cannot afford to alienate and exclude significant numbers of the poor, the black and the young.[8]

The consequences of social exclusion must now receive much more attention. The danger exists, and can be seen, that society will react negatively to the consequences of such exclusion. The justice system may be called upon to play a more repressive role, as can be seen in the current political competition to be tough on crime or show zero tolerance to the homeless and destitute. We must hold on to the need for policies that encourage social inclusion and the enfranchisement within the justice system of the poor. Will Hutton's marginalised and insecure groups were largely eligible for legal aid in 1979: now they are not. Current levels of civil legal aid eligibility are not acceptable: they need to be raised. Full legal aid in its traditional form must be more generally available to cover all those who are, by any reckoning, poor and not in a position to solve their own legal problems.

We need also to identify more precisely the composition of excluded groups. Twenty years ago, those still eligible for contributory legal aid were basically the working poor, many in steady but poorly paid jobs and often with families. The number of marginal groups will, however, now have expanded. Among them will be much better educated people, the young and unemployed or HIV and AIDS sufferers, for example. Also excluded will be the army of temporary workers and many of the self-employed, as discussed in the final section of this chapter. These groups may have enormous need of legal assistance but may have higher education and literacy skills. There may, therefore, be the opportunity for new services and new ways of delivering services to these groups: they may not need, at least for all their problems, the 'full service representation' traditionally available under legal aid. Nevertheless, their needs have to be addressed in any overall access to justice policy.

Access to justice

The concept of 'access to justice' is not unproblematic, although – or perhaps because – it has an almost universal political attraction. Lord Woolf and the Labour Party christened their reports with its name. The Liberal Democrat Lawyers Association followed suit. Even the Conservative government, eschewing it as title, nevertheless signed up for the idea by proclaiming in the very first paragraph of the green paper on legal aid:

> The aim of the Government is to improve access to justice.[9]

The attraction is an international phenomenon. The phrase has been used for reports on legal services in places as far apart as Australia and Quebec.

Few of these sources offer definitions or even underlying concepts. The phrase was designed as part of a politico-academic project. It asserts a broader approach than traditionally deployed by governments and was promulgated as a banner for a comprehensive assault on injustice:

> The access-to-justice approach tries to attack . . . barriers comprehensively, questioning the full array of institutions, procedures, and persons that characterize our judicial systems.[10]

A society with maximum access to justice is a society in which the exclusion from fair determination of rights and duties is not affected by the respective social, economic, political or other inequalities of the parties to any dispute. That requires an active battle against disadvantage. Testing for adequate access to justice means being able to select any potential inequality and being able to demonstrate that society has done its utmost to counteract its effect. Thus, we are not limited solely to the provision of representation for the unrepresented. We are concerned with the whole range of mechanisms to combat the disabling effects of sources of social exclusion such as racism, poverty, educational impoverishment and gender. The search is for ways of making constitutional rights real.

In a democracy, notions of justice and access to it are integrally linked to the political process. The deliberate rolling back of local government as a tier of real democratic decision-making has led to use of the legal system as an alternative forum. Disputes over rights to care in the community or educational services are now routinely fought out in the courts rather than town halls. The demise of collective trade union power has also encouraged the resolution of more disputes within the legal and justice structure.

The consequent widening role of litigation is often decried as regrettable. On the one hand, there was a widespread outcry by politicians and educationalists when a solicitor recently suggested that an education authority might be legally liable for failure to undertake its educational responsibilities. They seemed shocked that they might face a remedy with teeth that would actually require remedial action. On the other, the unpopularity of courts has inspired the search for alternatives and accounts for the attraction, at least within government, of alternative dispute resolution.

Antipathy to the courts raises an issue which must addressed. Culturally, we have tended to decry litigation and have sneered at our characterisation of what we saw as writ-happy North Americans. However, high litigation rates may well be a sign of an active citizenry, prepared to be vigilant as to their rights. Indeed, as economic and political forces reduce the scope for democratic decision-taking, we should expect rising levels of litigation. We should predict – and welcome – greater use of our civil justice system. If we are not getting it – and for the last few years litigation rates have been reducing – then that is more likely to be a sign of exclusion than of satisfaction. The increasing complexity of modern society should lead to a greater use of the law: when this does not happen, we should consider that something may be going wrong. Courts and lawyers may be too expensive or otherwise unavailable. This is not to say that we should not seek alternatives but we should not be content with reductions in litigation that arise from the despair and disadvantage of potential litigants.

Making access to justice a reality

We must reconceive our policies on access to justice. To do this, we should begin further back in the process than acceptance of legal aid in its current form and any pre-conceived limitations on its expenditure. Our aim should be a justice system which mediates conflict and governs society in a way acknowledged as legitimate by the widest possible range of interests.

We must seek to encourage the existence, and then meet the needs, of an active citizenry. We want a society in which its members seek redress for wrongs; are vigilant over their rights; and expect to acknowledge their responsibilities. We want a justice system which is devised to meet the needs, individually and collectively, of the society which it serves. To the extent that aspects of the system serve other needs at the expense of this goal it is dysfunctional.

We have to recognise the magnitude, even the impossibility, of the task that we set ourselves in seeking to reduce the inequalities necessarily generated in a complex society like our own to any kind of level playing field on which the poor and powerless are judged equally with the rich and powerful. The justice system cannot compensate for inequalities which a globalising and restructuring economy is almost bound to exacerbate. We must, however, do our best and recognise that we need to deploy all available mechanisms to meet our objective. The concept of access to justice was developed precisely to emphasise the need for a breadth of approach, identifying a wave of reform which:

> . . . includes, but goes *beyond advocacy*, whether inside or outside of the courts, and whether through governmental or private advocates. Its focus is on the full panoply of institutions and devices, personnel and procedures, used to process, and even prevent, disputes in modern societies.[11]

REFERENCES

1 Mr Justice Laws in *R v Lord Chancellor ex p Witham* (1997) *Times* 13 March, DC.
2 Ginsburg J delivering the US Supreme Court majority decision in *MLR v SLJ* on 16 December 1996.
3 Lord Woolf *Access to Justice: Interim Report* (HMSO, 1995), para 3.
4 Ibid, p17.
5 W Hutton *The State We're In* (Jonathan Cape, 1995), pp106–108.
6 C Oppenheim and L Harker *Poverty: the facts* (Child Poverty Action Group, 1996), p28.
7 Ibid, p167.
8 Speech, 24 November 1991.
9 Lord Chancellor's Department *Legal Aid – Targeting Need* (HMSO, 1995), Cm 2854, para 1.1.
10 M Cappelletti and B Garth *Access to Justice: Volume 1* (Sijthoff and Noordhof, 1978), p124.
11 Ibid, p49.

CHAPTER 2

Publicly funded legal and advice services 1945–1997

We are just about at the limit of what is possible without radical change.
Lord Mackay of Clashfern, Speech, 4 October 1991.

In speaking the words above to a meeting of legal aid practitioners in 1991, Lord Mackay has been proved right. In the event, little drastic reform was actually implemented during the Major government between 1992 and 1997. However, the groundwork was prepared for the radical change that Lord Mackay envisaged and which, in some form, is now unavoidable. This chapter provides the background for discussion of current options by tracing the development of publicly funded legal services since the Second World War.[1] An examination of the background to reform of civil justice is provided in *Achieving Civil Justice*.[2]

Publicly funded legal services are often regarded as synonymous with those provided by legal aid. Nevertheless, considerable advice and representation has been provided by agencies outside the legal aid system. From the 1970s, law centres have made an important contribution: throughout the whole period, and with growing impact over the last 20 years, there has been a strong lay advice movement within the voluntary sector. Other services, paid for privately, have also been relevant to the total pattern of provision. Trade unions have been an important source of legal services to their members. There are signs of an increasingly vigorous commercial paralegal sector. To create a manageable focus, this chapter concentrates, however, only on those services which are publicly funded.

The pattern of legal aid provision, with its attendant strengths and weaknesses, was set by the Rushcliffe Report in 1945. Conceived as the war was ending as one of a series of initiatives that amounted to the founding of the welfare state, this report recommended what North Americans came to call a 'judicare' system. This was based on the simple but powerful idea that lawyers should be available to the poor as they were to those who could afford them. The government advocated legislation for two reasons, both of which were important to the Law Society:

> ... to provide legal advice for those of slender means and resources so that no one will be financially unable to prosecute a just and reasonable claim or defend a legal right, and to allow counsel and solicitors to be remunerated for their services.[3]

Thus, legal aid was to be available in all courts or tribunals where lawyers normally appeared for private clients; eligibility should not be limited to those 'normally classed as poor' but extend to those of 'small or moderate means'. Above a free limit, there should be a sliding scale of contributions. In addition to this means test, there should be a test of merit, which for civil cases, would be judged by practitioners on a basis similar to that applied to private clients. Legal aid would be funded by the state but administered by the Law Society. The Lord Chancellor would be the responsible minister, assisted by an advisory committee. Means investigation of applicants would be undertaken by the National Assistance Board (whose tasks are now subsumed within the Department of Social Security). Finally, barristers and solicitors acting under legal aid should receive 'adequate' remuneration.

For the last 50 years, this model provided the framework within which legal aid developed. Three distinct periods can be identified. The first, between 1945 and 1970, saw the foundation of legal aid and, towards the end, the emergence of the first challenge to its structure, the law centre movement. The opening of the first law centre in London's North Kensington in 1970 provides, therefore, a convenient moment to identify the end of the first period and the beginning of second. This runs from 1970 to 1986, witnessing the absorption by the private profession of the law centre threat. By the end of this period, the threat from within (in the sense of within the community of practitioners) was being replaced by the threat from without: the government. 1986 was a pivotal year for the then Lord Chancellor, Lord Hailsham, initiated the first intended cuts to civil legal aid eligibility. This marked a new age in which government began to prioritise restraint of the budget, albeit in the face of unprecedented rises in cost. This third age can be appropriately seen as ending in 1997. Had the 1997 election returned a Conservative government, Lord

Mackay's white paper would have determined its approach, albeit that he himself announced his own retirement from office. In fact, Labour took office with a landslide majority, a looser commitment to future policies but with a determination to live within the Conservative spending estimates. Whatever happens in the future, 1997 will be seen as a turning point when the scheme established after the Second World War passed a decisive point in its reworking. The agenda inherited by the Labour government is discussed in the next chapter.

1945–1970: the opening phase

The origins of legal aid are buried deep in enlightened self-interest. The Rushcliffe Report represented an almost complete acceptance of the views of the Law Society. The Society needed an extension of legal aid, not least because it was concerned that its members would find it difficult to re-establish their practices after the war. In particular, it wanted to wind down the salaried divorce department which it had been forced to establish during the war. This represented too great a threat to private practice. The Society offered a discount on fees normally charged to paying clients in return for considerably more control of its members' destiny than was then being given to the medical profession in the newly proposed National Health Service.

The Rushcliffe committee rejected various alternatives which would have created a service delivered by salaried lawyers specifically oriented to the particular problems of the poor. Thus, out went the Haldane Society's plans to base legal aid on the thousand or so newly created citizens' advice bureaux – an idea that waited 40 years to return. So too did the submission of the Poor Man's Lawyer Associations (lawyers who gave advice from university-based settlements such as Toynbee Hall in the East End of London) calling for greater priority to be given to work with the Rent Restriction Acts, workmen's compensation, small claims and hire-purchase. The Law Society's priorities lay elsewhere. The scheme's first target was divorce work in the High Court. A gradual expansion into other areas of civil work followed and, in the early 1960s, legal aid became available in the county and, as significantly, magistrates' courts. Throughout the 1960s, criminal work expanded. By the end of this first period, overall expenditure was still low but the annual rate of expansion was over 50 per cent in terms of cost. However, in 1970 the legal aid scheme was still overwhelmingly concerned with the consequences of divorce and matrimonial problems.

Social welfare law (in the sense used throughout this book, follow-ing general usage within legal aid debate, of the law relating to land-lord and tenant, immigration, welfare benefits, consumer and debt, employment) was largely ignored. A 1969 survey of civil legal aid certificates in Birmingham found that 86 per cent related to family matters, nine per cent to accident claims and under five per cent for everything else.[4] The beginnings of an official unease could, however, be identified. In its 1969/70 annual report, the Lord Chancellor's Advisory Committee on Legal Aid argued for more attention to be given to the needs of people appearing before tribunals and called for 'some form of ancillary legal services'.

The Committee was responding to pressure for change. An alterna-tive model of publicly funded legal services was emerging from the United States. There, legal challenge had played an important part in the civil rights movement in the 1950s and 1960s. Legal services were accepted as an integral part of President Johnson's 'war against pov-erty'. In consequence, a new generation of radical lawyers emerged who spoke a heady language hitherto foreign to domestic debate:

> Our responsibility is to martial the forces of law and the strength of lawyers to combat the causes and effects of poverty. Lawyers must uncover the legal causes of poverty, remodel the systems which generate the cycle of poverty and design new social, legal and political tools and vehicles to move poor people from deprivation, depression and despair to opportunity, hope and ambition.[5]

The filtering of North American experience into Britain was given a major boost by the Society of Labour Lawyers' influential pamph-let, *Justice for All*, published in December 1968. This contained an appendix written by Michael Zander, then a young lecturer in law at the London School of Economics. He described the work of the US 'neighbourhood law firms'. The pamphlet argued for an establishment of similar organisations in this country. Virtually sim-ultaneously, the Committee of Conservative Lawyers published its proposals, *Rough Justice*, which demanded more planning of services and such innovations as grants for solicitors to set up in poor areas.[6]

This interest in radical reform reflected the political feeling of the age. Community-based groups were springing up; an innovative com-munity development programme was being developed to foster community action and experimented with use of the law; sociologists were 'rediscovering' poverty; an expanding higher education system enabled a broader range of students to encounter law. A gathering movement of law students, academics and practising lawyers, highly critical of the conservatism of the legal profession and the limitations of legal aid, became involved in a variety of informal legal advice provision. A flurry of legal advice projects sprung up, many using students or young lawyers to give assistance in inner city areas. From one of these in North Kensington emerged the first law centre. A group of people, including founder-lawyer Peter Kandler, had worked with a community organisation known as the Notting Hill People's Association, formed in part as a response to the 'gentrification' of this cosmopolitan area of London's inner city. A successful advice project in the summer of 1967 was eventually expanded into the first fully fledged law centre, which officially opened its doors on 17 July 1970, the day on which a new era of challenge can be dated to have commenced. The North Kensington Neighbourhood Law Centre was very much rooted in a practical response to the legal problems of its community. Its aim was to provide:

> . . . a first-class solicitors's service for the people of the North Kensington community; a service which is easily accessible, not intimidating, to which they can turn for guidance as they would to their family doctor, or as someone who can afford it would turn to his family solicitor.

The new movement did not have things all its own way. The Lord Chancellor asked his Legal Aid Advisory Committee to respond to the two political pamphlets. Its report, published in January 1970, represented a temporary setback to radical change.[7] The Committee was swayed by the Law Society's submission and followed its counter-recommendation for a new and flexible legal advice scheme, the beneficiary of which would be the private profession, and for law centres to be transferred to the direct control of the Law Society. Battle was engaged over what the Law Society and many of its high street practitioner members saw as a major threat to the established form of provision which they had dominated since 1945.

1970–1986: the middle period

Legal aid expanded throughout its second period, both in its range of schemes and in expenditure. The Law Society won its improved advice and assistance ('green form') scheme, whereby advice on any matter of English law was available on the basis of a simplified test of income and expenditure carried out by the solicitor. The Society also gradually expanded its duty solicitor schemes in the magistrates' courts. These emerged from being a voluntary initiative to being given a statutory basis in 1984. Then, in 1986, duty schemes were established for advice in the police station under the auspices of the Police and Criminal Evidence Act 1984. By 1986, total payments to the legal profession under all forms of legal aid was £419m; the net cost to the Exchequer (excluding client contributions and other costs recovered) was £342m. The cost of criminal legal aid had risen to well over half of the budget. The share of legal aid going on criminal cases in the magistrates' courts had doubled since 1969/70, now accounting for one-quarter of all legal aid costs.

The rise in the absolute cost of legal aid was reflected in its increasing importance to the legal profession. In 1970, legal aid had been a minor source of income. By the mid-1970s, its contribution could already be seen as significant in the figures for income from all sources which were provided to the Royal Commission on Legal Services. Figures for the mid- to late-1980s show that the trend had continued. Thus, legal aid represented seven per cent of the total fees of all solicitors in 1975/76; a decade later, in 1985/86, the equivalent percentage was 11.[8] The Bar's dependence (estimated at 30 per cent in 1977 by the Royal Commission) was even greater. Just over one-fifth of the Bar's total income came from criminal legal aid. Thus, legal aid helped to fund a major expansion of both branches of the profession in the 1970s and 1980s. During the 1970s, the Bar roughly doubled in size and the number of solicitors increased by about half.

A number of forces lay behind this expansion. Criminal work increased massively as representation in the magistrates' courts became the norm. In 1969, only one in five defendants appearing on indictable offences in magistrates' courts was represented under legal aid. By 1986, this had risen to an all-time high of over four-fifths. Also relevant was a soaring divorce rate: in 1968, the divorce rate stood at just under four per 1,000 marriages; in the two years following the Divorce Reform Act 1969, this grew to just over nine and by 1986 had reached a little under 13.[9] Legal aid for divorce itself was withdrawn in 1977, but the number of 'ancillary applications' relating to maintenance and children continued to rise. So too did the numbers of women seeking protection from domestic violence.

Another factor in the rise of expenditure was the rise in civil eligibility for legal aid introduced by the Labour government just before it lost office in 1979. From an initial 80 per cent of the population in 1950, eligibility on income grounds had slumped to 40 per cent by 1973. From this low point, eligibility on income grounds was increased to 79 per cent of the population in 1979. This returned legal aid to its initial high levels which it largely retained in the early 1980s, though it fell steadily throughout the decade.

The green form scheme had been advocated by the Law Society as a way of encouraging solicitors into the fields of social welfare law pioneered by the law centres. In fact, it was used largely to finance work in traditional fields of lawyers' activity – crime, family and personal injuries. Between them, these still accounted for half of the bills paid out in 1985/86. The slowness of this movement is shown by the figures from green form bills paid over the decade from 1975/76 to 1985/86. These indicate a growth from 27,000 to 172,000 of the number of green forms attributable to the 'social welfare law' areas of landlord and tenant, employment, hire-purchase and debt, welfare benefits and consumer. However, as a percentage of all green forms this represented only a rise in areas of social welfare law from 11 to 17 per cent.

The formation of the law centre in North Kensington was followed by others, initially in London but soon in the provinces, that began to operate in the early 1970s. The Law Society hoped to control the emergent centres by way of conditions attached to the terms on which law centre solicitors could work, through 'waivers' of the professional rules then existing against advertising and sharing fees. In its 1973/74 report on the legal aid scheme, the Law Society savaged law centres for 'stirring up political and quasi-political confrontation far removed from ensuring equal access to the protection of the law'.

By 1975, the Law Society had worked itself into a position where it acceded to pressure from a group of local solicitors in Hillingdon outraged by the imminent funding of a local law centre. It tried to stop solicitors practising in the centre by refusing them the necessary waivers, on the ground that local solicitors met local need for services. The subsequent political impasse resulted in the intervention of the Labour Lord Chancellor, Lord Elwyn Jones, and the Society's undignified retreat under the threat of legislation. The Law Society and the law centres reached an accommodation, negotiated under pressure from the Lord Chancellor, that suited both. Provided that the centres did not compete with private practice in its traditional areas (such as adult crime, matrimonial work, personal injury, probate or conveyancing) the Law Society would grant the necessary permissions. By the time of its evidence to the Royal Commission on Legal Services in 1979, the Society had come round to the view that, far from being a threat, law centres generated work for private practice.

As one source of threat to the emergent law centre movement receded, another took its place. Although the second half of the 1970s saw steady growth overall in the number of law centres, all was not well. From early on, there were danger signals in relation to finance. As early as 1975, soon after the election of the Labour government that was to last until 1979, the Lord Chancellor had instituted central government funding of eight centres which were in financial difficulties. Numbers eventually peaked in the mid-1980s at 62. The Conservative government elected in 1979 maintained the funding commitment of the previous administration to the eight centres then grant-aided but sought refuge from further commitment in the line that law centres should be funded by local authorities. Some were prepared to do so but, alas, the majority were not. In consequence, law centres never became a large enough force to dominate the mainstream of publicly funded legal services. They survived on the periphery, in relatively small numbers and with, in most cases, very low levels of local government funding.

Law centres were not the only beneficiary of the expansion of local authorities' role and funding in the 1970s and 1980s. A vigorous advice sector emerged, spearheaded by the citizens advice bureaux (CABx). These were established during the Second World War and then neglected. As the 1970s began, they increasingly found favour with local authorities. Their numbers almost doubled between the mid-1960s and the mid-1980s (from 473 in 1966 to 869 in 1986) and the volume of enquiries more than quadrupled (from 1.3m to 6.8m in the same period). In addition, several hundred independent advice centres were set up. There was also a gradual development of local authority funded specialist services, some within the voluntary sector but some within local authorities themselves, mainly operating in the fields of housing, social security or debt.

The advice sector experimented to a small extent with the employment of lawyers. The first combined CAB and law centre opened in Paddington in 1973, followed by a similar venture in Hackney in 1976. Community lawyers, who both advised on individual problems and trained lay advisers within the bureaux, were appointed to CABx in North Kensington, Lewisham and Waltham Forest. By 1977, ten CABx employed lawyers and the National Association of CABx resolved to develop more posts. The CAB service developed the idea of resource lawyers who would assist the overwhelmingly lay workforce of the bureaux. In the 1970s, there had been periods when a degree of rivalry with law centres was apparent. However, by the 1980s, it looked as if the advice sector and law centres had embarked on different courses.

The ferment of political activity and critical analysis of the legal profession led the Labour government to establish a Royal Commission on Legal Services in 1976, chaired by an accountant, Sir Henry, soon to be Lord, Benson. This initiative had been resisted by the then Lord Chancellor, Lord Elwyn-Jones, because he feared that it would act as a brake on reform. His political antennae were correct: the Commission's report, published in October 1979, was almost universally regarded as unexciting and unoriginal. Furthermore, the Labour government had by then lost power. In retrospect, the Commission was probably established a decade too early. Legal services did require major reform but the necessity of making difficult decisions was not yet sufficiently apparent. Both the Bar and the Law Society were able to maintain the *status quo*.

On the legal profession, the Commission was profoundly conservative. There was to be no challenge to the privileges of solicitors or barristers. On legal aid, the Commission was worthy but dull. Eligibility for civil legal aid should be raised but the Law Society should retain administrative control. In relation to law centres and salaried services, the Commission appeared almost hostile. While acknowledging that:

> ... the impact of law centres has been out of all proportion to their size, to the number of lawyers who work in them and to the amount of work it is possible for them to undertake ...[10]

the Commission argued:

> ... the time has come to move forward from a period of experiment to one of consolidation, characterised by continuity, orderly development, adequate resources and proper administrative and financial control.[11]

Law centres were to be transposed into more manageable and managed citizens law centres.[12] The Commission was also conservative on the role of the advice sector. The citizens advice bureaux should stay in their place:

> ... the division of function between the para-legal work of the CAB service and the use of professional lawyers has hitherto been established on a sensible and practical basis and it should continue in this way. We do not think that a CAB [Advice Bureau] should build up, as part of its staff, a team of lawyers to give legal advice to individuals.[13]

The demise of the Labour government meant that the Commission's vision was never tested and we do not know whether its recommendations would have been implemented. The incoming Conservative government largely ignored them and went about its business. More benignly than might have been predicted, the incoming Conservative administration did not take an overtly hostile view of law centres. Lord Hailsham, reappointed Lord Chancellor in 1979, simply insisted that funding responsibility should remain with local rather than central government. Since Conservative local authorities were, largely but not exclusively, somewhat reluctant to fund law centres, they became increasingly identified with Labour local authorities and the most financially secure were to be found in authorities which remained Labour throughout the 1980s and 1990s. Overall, throughout the 1970s and early 1980s, local authorities were more impressed by the claims of advice agencies than law centres. Funding and numbers expanded massively. In London, the late flowering of a left-wing administration at the Greater London Council spearheaded a positive flood of funding for advice agencies in general and welfare benefits work.

By 1986, the government was ready to seek advantage of this expanding advice provision in terms of a bold proposal, advanced in an 'Efficiency Scrutiny', that large areas of the green form legal advice and assistance scheme be transferred to the voluntary advice sector. In the event, after fierce debate, the recommendation was scuppered by a reluctant, though tempted, CAB service. But the agenda for more government intervention was set. The main immediate effect of the scrutiny was administrative. It laid the ground for the transfer of legal aid administration from the Law Society to the Legal Aid Board. On the one hand, this was a technical and overdue recognition of the proper roles of government and profession. In another, it marked a defining moment and the beginning of a new era. This became particularly obvious when Lord Hailsham announced in February 1986 the first major cut to entitlement, the slashing of dependants' additions by 17 per cent. LAG's monthly journal, *Legal Action*, noted at the time:

> The latest move has provoked additional concern because it shows that rather than reform or rationalise the system, the Government prefers to attack the intended beneficiaries of legal aid.[14]

1986–1997: entering the endgame

Debate on legal aid since the mid-1980s has been increasingly dominated by its cost. Lord Mackay's period in office culminated first in a green paper on legal aid and then a white paper in which he sought to address this overriding problem. The content of these is discussed later (see p36) because implementation of any reform was left to his successors. The rise in cost from the mid-1980s is, on any basis, striking. Legal aid has suffered a 'costs blow out'. In 1985–86, expenditure was £319m. In 1995–96, total expenditure was £1.4bn made up of £675m for civil legal aid; £530m for criminal; and £272m for advice and assistance.[15] In the decade between 1986–87 and 1995–96, the average annual rise in expenditure topped 16 per cent. For three years between 1990–91 and 1992–93, annual rises were 20 per cent a year with that for the middle year, 1991–92, reaching almost to a third in a single year.[16] These rises far outstripped the number of bills paid. During the critical period in the early 1990s, these were increasing at roughly half the rate of total expenditure. Government concern was understandable.

One cause of these increases, though minor within the total picture, was greater involvement by solicitors in advice and assistance in general and for areas of social welfare law in particular. Overall, advice given under the green form scheme has risen by around a half over the last decade.

TABLE 1: LEGAL ADVICE AND ASSISTANCE 1986–87 AND 1996–97[17]		
	1986–87	*1996–97*
Total number of bills paid	980,507	1,531,972

Those covering social welfare law have expanded at a significantly higher rate (see TABLE 2, opposite).

Thus, the overall growth in civil non-matrimonial legal advice has been doubling over the last decade, a higher rate of increase than for legal advice generally. The rise has not been constant over all areas. In particular, advice in immigration/nationality and welfare benefits has grown disproportionately. The first fact probably reflects greater tightening of the relevant legislation and more sophistication by lawyers in response. The second is perhaps more dubious. Solicitors are undoubtedly giving much more welfare benefits advice and a significant number of firms have hired welfare benefits workers from the voluntary sector to do so. The quality and depth of this advice is, however, unknown.

As Lord Chancellor, Lord Mackay broadened the response to expenditure rises. In addition to eligibility cuts he made a determined

TABLE 2: LEGAL ADVICE AND ASSISTANCE
(NON-MATRIMONIAL CIVIL CASES) 1986–87 AND 1996–97

	Number of bills paid	
	1986–87	1996–97
Immigration and nationality	7,823	67,175
Consumer	21,138	34,261
Welfare benefits	28,823	165,416
Employment	19,924	20,446
Hire-purchase and debt	57,529	86,730
Accidents and injuries	44,575	77,188
Landlord/tenant, housing	60,672	114,775
Other	115,788	178,945
Total	356,272	744,936

move to introduce standard fees so that increases in total cost might at least be more in line with increases in cases. By the mid-1990s, this was broadly the case. Crime was, more or less, protected: the cuts were made to eligibility to legal advice where contributory levels of qualification were totally removed and the scheme reduced to bedrock eligibility at income support rates. Also in the firing line was civil legal aid (see TABLE 3).

TABLE 3: PERCENTAGE OF HOUSEHOLDS ELIGIBLE FOR
CIVIL LEGAL AID ON INCOME GROUNDS[18]

	%
1979–80	77
1992–93	53
1993–94	48
1994–95	47

Estimates by at least one independent statistician suggest an even more dramatic fall.[19] There is evidence that legal aid is increasingly available only to those with income at the lowest levels.

Not only was eligibility slashed. Those who qualified subject to contributions had to pay them at a higher rate and for a longer period. The result was predictable. Legal aid became increasingly a benefit available only to the poorest, largely synonymous with those in receipt of basic social security means-tested benefits. Thus, the percentage of recipients that are required to pay a contribution, which would reflect higher incomes, has dropped significantly over the last 30 years. By 1996–97, 7.5 per cent of all those offered legal aid were liable for contributions at an annual rate of £500 or more.

TABLE 4: PERCENTAGE OF ALL CIVIL LEGAL AID
CERTIFICATES WHICH ARE GRANTED ON THE BASIS
OF NO CONTRIBUTION FROM THE RECIPIENT

	All courts %	All except magistrates' courts %	Magistrates' courts only %
1962–63		49	79
1973–74	78		
1983–84	78		
1986–87	80		
1996–97	85		

The human stories behind these figures were revealed in a research study for the Legal Aid Board:

> Those who received other state benefits felt that their contributions were particularly unfair. A divorced mother of two children said, 'if you are on family credit of £46 per week, to find £91 a month is impossible'. A mother of two receiving invalidity and child benefit who was seeking maintenance from her ex-husband told us, 'if I had £47 per month I wouldn't need to chase maintenance' ... An unemployed man who fractured a foot on an uneven pavement said his diet consisted mainly of beans at 7p a can. His only income was invalidity benefit of £2,307 a year, and his contribution was assessed at £23.80 a month.[20]

The CAB service found similar stories from among the clients consulting them.[21] In these circumstances, the proposals in Lord Mackay's white paper on legal aid to increase further the contributions payable seem singularly ill-advised.

Law centres did not share equally with the private profession in the increased volume of work undertaken in social welfare law over the last decade. In 1986, there were 56 law centres; there are currently 53 in England and Wales, though more in Scotland and one in Northern Ireland. The amount of money received by law centres for green form work has risen from just over £1m in 1990–91 to £1.8m in 1996–97. This rate of rise has, however, been dwarfed by the increased funds received by agencies that would define themselves as within the advice sector but which have employed lawyers to take advantage of the ability to claim legal aid. Their income from legal advice and assistance has risen from £202,000 to £1.9m over the same period. In addition, the Legal Aid Board dispersed another £2m to advice agencies without lawyers as part of its non-solicitor agencies pilot project. As a result, law centres no longer receive, as a group within the not-for-profit sector, the majority of Legal Aid Board funding. In 1990–91 law centres received £2.1m out of the £2.4m dispersed. By 1996–97, they received only £3.7m of the total £8.2m paid by the Board to all not-for-profit organisations.

Thus, law centres are no longer the major providers of legal case-work within the not-for-profit sector. First, private practitioners, many transferring from law centres, have rushed into the vacuum created by the low level of provision and the high level of need. Special interest groups, largely dominated by private practitioners are now powerful forces within the field. Organisations like the Housing Law Practitioners Association or the Immigration Law Practitioners Association have memberships overwhelmingly from the private sector. Leading experts in emergent areas of social welfare law, such as education or community care, are also to be found in private practice. Second, the advice sector is picking up speed, as is reflected in its legal aid income. Even though most of its legal aid money is for advice, not-for-profit organisations which are not designated as law centres, received around £383m in 1996–97 as costs in relation to civil legal aid, creeping to just over a third of that paid to law centres. Third, high level test cases, certainly in the field of public law, though still taken by law centres, have become much more a specialism of national not-for-profit pressure groups such as the Public Law Project, Shelter, the Child Poverty Action Group and Liberty. These are organisations with national constituencies from which the law centres demarcate themselves by reference to their orientation to their local community.

The centres can still prove effective. They have given a high priority to serving ethnic minority communities that may otherwise find it difficult to find help. Particularly impressive, for example, is the statistic that no less than 47 per cent of all the 13,000 people advised by Central London Community Law Centre were from Chinese or Vietnamese origin. Evidence of effective outreach of this kind can be found in many law centre reports. A survey of North Islington clients found that 17 per cent were of Black Caribbean origin and a similar percentage Black African as compared with local populations of 5 and 3 per cent respectively according to the most recent census information. Furthermore, law centres can make striking use of the range of responses open to them. An example was provided by the poll tax, an unpopular tax introduced by the Conservative government which led in 1989 to a flood of cases in which those who, for one reason or other, had not paid the tax were threatened with imprisonment. Centres such as Leicester and Bradford mobilised on an impressive scale to provide representation; produce literature; spearhead tactics.[22] Centres have also participated in campaigns with a test case component as exemplified by Humberside's involvement in the benefit rights of seafarers made redundant in the mid-1980s and Hillingdon and Camden's participation in the issue of sex discrimination.

In overall numbers, law centres are dwarfed by the number of advice agencies. In 1995–96, 900 organisations were members of the Federation of Independent Advice Centres. The CAB service had over 700 separate bureaux as members with over 1,000 outlets. Even Shelter, the housing pressure group, had 30 local centres. The national government grant for the National Association of Citizens Advice Bureaux was £12m, compared with a Legal Aid Board grant to the Law Centres Federation of £67,000. The volume of advice given is similarly high. Citizens advice bureaux dealt with 6.5m problems brought to them by 5.3m people. The advice sector in general and the CAB service in particular is as diverse, within itself, as are law centres. Agencies range from those with part-time managers and opening hours to linked bureaux within a conurbation almost entirely staffed by full-timers, some of whom may be lawyers. The strength of the advice sector is probably the reason why this country has not developed a network of centrally funded law centres to resemble the community legal clinics in Ontario or the community legal centres in Australia.

Involvement of the voluntary sector was very much one of the projects of the Legal Aid Board, with enormous implications for the development of service delivery. More immediately important to mainstream legal aid practice was the Board's approach to quality. This reflected the early domination of Board membership by people from industrial and commercial backgrounds, in particular its first chairman, John Pitts. They imported the doctrine of 'preferred suppliers', the development of an identified group of providers of service with whom the Board agreed quality levels and with whom the Board would work co-operatively. The Board developed the idea of 'franchis-ing' legal aid provision, initially in relation to advice. In its original form, it was presented as benignly non-exclusive:

> ... a system that would involve identifying those who can satisfy criteria of competence and reliability and to assist and encourage them by freeing them from some of the restrictions now applying to legal aid.[23]

As the Board developed its ideas, using a pilot with solicitors' firms in Birmingham, it identified three major areas in which quality could be measured. It described these in its 1991–92 annual report and they have changed little since, save for the beginnings of an additional concern with what are known as 'outcome' measures on which consultants have been engaged to examine possible approaches (eg, statistical comparisons of success, client satisfaction measurements). The main measures were to be:

(a) ... the general management and organisation of the practice or agency, covering such matters as supervision, training, file manage-ment and recording systems etc;

(b) ... the quality of work submitted by the practice or agency to the Board, eg legal aid applications, bills, etc; and

(c) most importantly ... the work done directly for the client, that is in the collection of information from the client and the advice given in the light of that information.[24]

As implemented, adequate performance of these measures was gauged by visits to applicants' firms and measurement of their per-formance, in turn, on three separate areas of performance. First, gen-eral management was measured against compliance with Practice Management Standards which the Legal Aid Board cajoled out of the Law Society. These were advisory for all solicitors but made manda-tory by the franchising specification for those wishing to have fran-chises.[25] They covered such matters, standard for many businesses but revolutionary for many lawyers, as implementation of proper staff appraisal systems, induction procedures for new staff and properly constructed business and service plans. Second, solicitors' com-petence at form-filling was easily measured by the Board. Third, the Board sought to measure directly the performance of solicitors in relation to their clients by picking files at random and measuring the procedural approach adopted against a standard list, allowing a per-centage score of performance to be calculated by a non-lawyer. These 'transaction criteria' were devised by a group of academic consult-ants.[26] The criteria remain controversial, though undoubtedly they do allow a form of measurement of how well files are kept against some concept of a norm.

The Board has, certainly until recently, resisted any implementation of peer review for the reasons set out by their consultants:

> ... peer review would be an expensive part of any quality assurance system. The use of lawyer assessors is likely to be prohibitive in cost terms. Furthermore a uniform system of assessment would still have to be designed to articulate assessment criteria to be used by different lawyer assessors.[27]

Such hesitancy contrasts with the approach of the CAB service. Its national association (NACAB) has undertaken two recent studies of the quality of the work undertaken by its bureaux. Both were highly critical of standards; both effectively questioned the extent to which advice agencies could provide adequate legal services; both were perceived as highly embarrassing for the service; neither were published and both were leaked into the public domain. However, both are important for all these reasons and because they demonstrated a different approach to quality measurement from that adopted by the Legal Aid Board. As a service provider, NACAB was concerned with the substance of its advice not only the observance of procedures. One study was on housing advice and the other on employment. In both, the researchers made a direct assessment of quality. The results and implications were noted in a study made on behalf of the Legal Aid Board:

> Not only do these two studies shed important light on the quality of service actually provided and how advice workers go about the task of giving advice, but they also provide a different approach to assessing the quality of advice work:
>
> > the quality of advice in 319 cases was looked at by an employment lawyer with extensive experience of working with CABx. The cases were marked to a standard of competence that would be required to meet NACAB general advice standards and to protect against negligence. The cases were marked according to a scale of 'good', 'passable', 'poor' and 'very poor' and against specific criteria: diagnosis; accuracy; options, consequences and limitations; appropriateness; timeliness; effectiveness and information collection.[28]

The study, thus, has two important points to offer. First, it underlines the significant problems in seeking to use non-lawyers to deliver adequate legal services and provides an introduction to a hitherto underconsidered distinction: that between general and legal advice. Second, it is a major contribution to the experience of how to measure quality. The two studies illustrate the possibility of undertaking structured analysis of the quality of casework and are better, therefore, as ultimate indicators of judgment than the more indirect approaches favoured by the Legal Aid Board.

Franchising's progress has been affected by its origin as a development of the 1986 Efficiency Scrutiny's approach to legal advice. As at April 1997, a total of 1,740 offices (out of a total of around 12,000 that are paid for legal aid work during a year) had a franchise for at least one area of work. An early row erupted when the Legal Aid Board revealed that it had a target of around 2,500 firms. The absolute number of franchises is still low but, since it includes the larger providers, begins to approach the originally envisaged numbers.

The Legal Aid Board has conducted two pilot programmes into the use of not-for-profit agencies. The first was a relatively minor project using grants to law centres and other agencies to explore various alternative methods of delivering services. This was really too superficial to provide much useful information. Money was spread around projects as diverse as a telephone consultancy service, an environmental project and assistance to a national pressure group in identifying test cases. This research was somewhat underwhelming in its findings: it was not actually clear that the law centres had done very much with their money, perhaps because of the artificiality of the time-limited project.[29]

The more important project, about to move into a second and larger phase, was an experiment to see whether advice agencies could, as recommended by the Efficiency Scrutiny back in 1986, deliver legal advice. This has been claimed to be an enormous success and the advice agencies are being wooed to continue their participation. However, the research on the pilot identified that legal advice eligibility is now so low that more than a third of people interviewed by the 42 pilot agencies were ineligible (only 62 per cent would have qualified).[30] It is also apparent that the agencies undertake relatively low level work. Of the closed cases in the pilot agencies, only the following percentages involved any assistance beyond giving immediate advice: welfare benefits – 19; immigration – 10; housing – 26; employment – 17; debt – 42; consumer – 8.[31] Further study is required to indicate how this pattern compares with other providers.

1997 and beyond: the future

A government of any persuasion would be forced to implement fundamental reform of legal aid. Lord Mackay's green and white papers provided careful preparation for what a re-elected Conservative administration would have done. The next chapter discusses the competing agendas that face the Labour ministerial team as they approach the question of the extent to which policy should be developed.

REFERENCES

1 This chapter is a revision of Chapter 2 of *A Strategy for Justice* (LAG, 1992) and may, accordingly, strike regular readers of LAG material as familiar.

2 R Smith (ed) *Achieving Civil Justice: appropriate dispute resolution for the 1990s* (LAG, 1996), Chapter 1.

3 Lord Chancellor *Summary of the Proposed New Service* Cmnd 7563 (HMSO, 1948) quoted in National Audit Office *Report by the Comptroller and Auditor General: Lord Chancellor's Department: Provision of Legal Aid in England and Wales* (HMSO, 1986), para 2.2.

4 L Bridges, B Sufrin, J Whetton and R White *Legal Services in Birmingham* (Birmingham University, 1975).

5 Quoted in J Handler, E Hollingsworth and R White *Lawyers and the Pursuit of Legal Rights* (Academic Press Inc, 1978), p5.

6 Society of Labour Lawyers *Justice for All* (Fabian Research Pamphlet No 273, 1968) and Society of Conservative Lawyers *Rough Justice* (SCL, 1968).

7 *Report of the Advisory Committee on the Better Provision of Legal Advice and Assistance (1985–86)* (HMSO, 1986), HC 87.

8 *Royal Commission on Legal Services Final Report* Cmnd 7648 (HMSO, 1979), Vol 1, para 36.81, and C Glasser, 'Financing legal services' (1988) *Law Society's Gazette* 20 April.

9 L Stone *Road to Divorce: England 1530–1987* (Oxford University Press, 1990), Table 13.1, p436.

10 *Royal Commission on Legal Services Final Report* Cmnd 7648 (HMSO, 1979), Vol 1, para 8.11.

11 Ibid, para 8.13.

12 Ibid, paras 8.17–8.30.

13 Ibid, para 7.25.

14 March 1986 *Legal Action* 3.

15 Lord Chancellor's and Law Officers Departments *The Government's Expenditure Plans 1996–97 to 1998–99* Cm 3209 (HMSO, 1996), p25.

16 *The Government's Expenditure Plans 1991–92 to 1993–94* and *1994–95 to 1996–97* Cm 1510 and Cm 2509 (HMSO, 1991 and 1994).
17 Legal Aid Board *37th Annual Reports 1986–87* (HMSO, 1988), p39 and Legal Aid Board *Annual Report 1996–97* (HMSO, 1997), p98.
18 *Hansard*, Written Answer 21 April 1994, col 590.
19 M Murphy 'Civil legal aid eligibility estimates', published as Appendix 1 to *A Strategy for Justice* (LAG, 1992), p161.
20 R Woolfson and J Plotnikoff *Report of study into reasons for refusal of offers of contributory civil legal aid* (Legal Aid Board, 1996), p15–16.
21 See *Barriers to Justice: CAB clients' experience of legal services* (NACAB, 1995), p20–22.
22 See further J Richardson 'Law Centres experience of information work' in R Smith(ed) *Shaping the Future: new directions in legal services* (LAG, 1996), pp118–121.
23 Legal Aid Board *Second Stage Consultation on the Future of the Green Form Scheme* (May 1989), p6.
24 Ibid, p24.
25 See the published version, Legal Aid Board *Franchising Specification* (July 1993).
26 See A Sherr, R Moorhead and A Paterson *Lawyers – The Quality Agenda Volumes one and two* (Legal Aid Board, July 1994).
27 Ibid, p17.
28 J Steele and G Bull *Fast, Friendly and Expert? Legal Aid Franchising in Advice Agencies without Solicitors* (Policy Studies Institute, 1996), p59.
29 G Bull and J Sergeant *Alternative Methods of Delivering Services* (Policy Studies Institute, 1996), p52.
30 J Steele and G Bull *Fast, Friendly and Expert? Legal Aid Franchising in Advice Agencies without Solicitors* (Policy Studies Institute, 1996), p87.
31 Ibid, p46.

CHAPTER 3

Competing agendas

Justice is one of the foundations on which the next Labour government will build.

Labour *Access to Justice* (1995), p1.

Government policy on legal services should be built upon the foundations of justice. But, as the quotation above recognises, there are other considerations which compete for attention and whose power must be recognised. This chapter considers two: the administrative agenda and the practitioner agenda.

As the history of legal aid shows, governments have until recently adopted an almost uniquely 'hands off' attitude. The legal profession has been allowed to dominate the form and structure of legal aid since the Second World War and has obtained immeasurably more favourable treatment than doctors, brought into the National Health Service on a largely salaried basis. Until 1989, the Law Society actually administered most of it. Escalating expenditure has forced change and Lord Mackay, as Conservative Lord Chancellor for a decade from 1987, saw through a programme of reform designed to take over greater administrative control as a prelude to greater financial control. The Legal Aid Board was created to drive this agenda onward.

The drive for administrative control impacted on practitioners. Neither the Bar nor the Law Society appreciated attempts to curb the incomes of their members. By contrast, other potential providers saw their chance. Some parts of the advice sector seized gleefully on the possibilities of central government funding. This was particularly welcome because the advice sector's traditional funding source, local government, was coming under increasing financial pressure.

Consequently, the practitioner agenda in publicly funded legal services is fairly clear: at stake is the livelihood of a considerable workforce distributed through both branches of the legal profession and increasingly to be found in the voluntary sector.

The administrative agenda

Lord Mackay expressed high hopes of the Legal Aid Board that was to be the 'centrepiece'[1] of the legislation that became the Legal Aid Act 1988. The Board was 'to achieve a central strategic role for legal aid'[2] and it has not disappointed. The Board has rapidly assumed such a powerful position in relation to policy that it stands poised to dominate the future, almost irrespective of government. This puts the Board in an interesting, and occasionally difficult, constitutional position, somewhat at odds with the original understanding of Lord Mackay:

> The Legal Aid Board is not going to be free to do what is likes, when it likes and how it likes with the legal aid scheme . . . The Government will continue to set the broad framework of the legal aid arrangements . . . [3]

Things have, in the event, worked out rather differently, in part due to the strength of the Board and in part to the weakness of the Lord Chancellor's Department. The Board's command of its brief; its business-dominated approach; its possession of the empirical detail of legal aid and its sheer effectiveness have given it a lead role in policy-making. Much of this strength flows from the force of character of its chief executive since its beginning, Steve Orchard. Much continues to depend on his dominant personality. This has established a distinct institutional role for the Board. It has, in practice therefore, become much more akin to bodies in other jurisdictions (such as exist in New Zealand, Australia and some provinces of Canada) where its equivalents have greater statutory autonomy. As Lord Mackay made clear, this was not intended to be the domestic constitutional model. However, since the Board's establishment, the Lord Chancellor's Department has responded to, rather than directed, policy debate. This has created a relationship which is not always easy. At times, the Lord Chancellor's Department has appeared to be floundering in maintaining anything more than a formal control of the Board's initiatives and rubber-stamping its proposals.

The success of the Board in improving legal aid's administration,

though still not perfect, must be acknowledged. The Legal Aid Board
hit the ground running with wave after wave of reform designed to
modernise and improve legal aid administration. It is a tribute to its
effectiveness that few solicitors, critics though they may be of the
Board's detailed performance, argue that they would prefer to return
to the days when their own Law Society administered legal aid.
Memories of its failure are still too recent. The former administration
reached its nadir in the service offered to legal aid practitioners in the
south London area. An ill-considered attempt to introduce a paper-
less office floundered as microfiche machines drowned in paper that
they were not powerful enough to process.

The Board's tough administrative stance gives it a political cred-
ibility. Its views on how legal aid costs can be 'brought under
control' have been highly influential. Indeed, its response to the
government's green paper may prove to be as important as any other
policy paper produced by government, opposition or anyone else.[4]
The Board's ace is its empirical control of information and its
practical position as executor of any policy: its judgment of what is
possible or impossible naturally carries considerable weight. In effect,
the theoretical division between policy and administration, as
advanced by the Conservative government in its creation of administrative agencies, is reversed. The Board controls policy because it
controls administration.

The Board moved rapidly from overhauling its internal administration to reforming its external relationships with solicitors. As a result,
its creation, franchising, has effectively become the only game in
town. Debate tends to become limited to the detail of the content of
the franchise, rather than any broader discussion. This imports a
significant distortion which is not really the Board's fault but is the
consequence of the lack of a wider political context.

The Board's political agenda is unavoidably administration-driven:
it is not necessarily linked to policy considerations about, for
example, the desirable scope of, and eligibility for, services. The
Board has sold its basic package hard, arguing that the way forward is
to link franchises with regional budgets and a series of separate
funds. Expenditure will be contained because the number and price
of the franchises will be matched to the amount in the funds. With
regional budgets come regional legal services committees to advise on
regional priorities. The Board's pivotal position in terms of future
development was consolidated by its achievement in getting the Lord
Chancellor and his department to recognise the importance of piloting reform prior to full implementation. Hence, it has considerable

say in the establishment and analysis of developments. The Board has, thus, taken a lead role in setting up pilots to explore new proposals.

The Board's 'can do' style is undoubtedly refreshing and contrasts with the traditionally quiet complacency that might be fairly said to have dominated many of the other preserves of the Lord Chancellor's Department. The Courts Service has, for example, proved much less dynamic. The Board shows the benefit of vigorous leadership both from its senior executives and its members. There are, however, the well-worn dangers of too much haste. The Board's drive for results sometimes appears to encourage the cutting of significant corners in the dash for reform. For example, there is evidence that consultants, supposedly hired for their independence, have been too aware of the Board's desires. Behold, the observations of the Policy Studies Institute on the relative cost of non-lawyers and lawyers, a key issue on which the Board has hinged a major policy initiative in seeking to shift legal aid monies to the not-for-profit sector. Its researchers were incautious enough to conclude in their interim report:

> At this stage in the pilot the cost of providing services through non-solicitor agencies appears to be less than through solicitors.[5]

The PSI's final report revealed the level of computational gymnastics required to sustain such a conclusion:

> We can calculate an equivalent [to solicitors] hourly rate for non-solicitor agencies by dividing the estimated cost of the caseworker resource by the target of 1,100 hours .... However, ... figures are based on agencies' own estimates of costs . . . It should also be noted that an output of 1,100 hours is not actually being achieved in all cases.[6]

In other words, the calculation depends on unverified assertions of cost and fictional estimates of time. A similar criticism might be made of the development of transaction criteria as a quality measure.[7]

The Board may also have suffered from being taken too much at its word in terms of what is to be done. It is now carrying an enormous weight of expectation. Singlehandedly, the Board is being expected to come up with the answer to quality control of legal and mediation services; service delivery by lawyers and lay advisers; and the development from scratch of a nationally operating series of matrimonial mediation services. Each one of these raises major methodological questions which are in danger of being left unanswered in the intemperate rush for immediate results. By 1997, the Board was involved in the establishment of contracting projects in mediation; block funding of legal aid in family and matrimonial cases; advice provision by not-for-profit agencies; block funding of advice by solicitors and contracting of criminal legal advice and assistance, including court and police station duty solicitors. In addition, it was planning to take over means assessment from a unit of the Department of Social Security and to replace its outdated computer system. Such a workrate is commendable though there must be some concern as to whether quality can match quantity, somewhat of an irony for an organisation that first set out its stall in the quality assurance marketplace.

There was little contradiction between the Board and its constitutional master during Lord Mackay's period of office. The Board's drive for administrative control of the legal aid budget was fuelled by Lord Mackay's increasing urgency to find a way to restrict cost. It became apparent that more was required to do this than the random scattergun approach of contingent cuts to eligibility, scope and remuneration originally marshalled by the Lord Chancellor's Department as the first lines of attack. The extent to which any government will be forced to change existing arrangements can be seen in the estimates of future legal aid expenditure released with the budget in November 1996. Labour has announced that it would implement all government spending targets for 1996/97 and live within its overall spending total in the following year. Hence, the acceptance of these figures requires any government to deliver long-term fundamental restructuring. The administrative agenda is set, necessarily, to dominate the next period of legal aid's development.

The Conservative government announced its own plans for fundamental reform in the white paper published in the summer of 1996. Ignoring the somewhat liberal approach of its earlier green paper, this proposed fashioning legal aid provision in accordance with certain key political shibboleths. The difference in tone and substance between green and white paper is striking enough to illustrate either a considerable hardening of attitude or a somewhat more cynical attempt to manipulate opinion through an initial soft sell. Many in the advice sector, for example, found tempting the blandishments that the green paper had offered. It turned out that they had been conned. A key substantive difference was that the first proposed extending legal aid tribunals; the second rejected the idea.

The main elements of the government's proposals, as set out in *Striking the Balance*,[8] were threefold. First, franchising was to be combined with the idea of a 'hard cap' for legal aid overall and individually for crime, family and civil cases by way of a myriad of subfunds from which practitioners would bid for resources. By this means, it hoped to drive down prices and limit total expenditure. Client eligibility on merits grounds would be controlled by a matrix of national and regional guidelines, established by the Lord Chancellor and as advised by the newly created regional legal services committees. Second, legal aid would be available for funding a range of competing providers, not just lawyers. Money would be diverted to mediators in family cases (a proposal trailed in matrimonial legislation the year previously) and to advice agencies who would be cheaper than solicitors for some types of advice. Third, the financial liability of legally aided litigants would be increased. In civil cases, unsuccessful litigants would be liable for the costs of their opponents. A new range of contributions would become payable in both civil and criminal cases.

Lord Irvine has stated that 'the White Paper is a dead letter'.[9] However, Labour's acceptance of the expenditure estimates limits the differences possible in policy. Certain trends are unavoidable, whatever the detail of the reforms to come. Legal aid practitioners will become a much more differentiated sector of the legal profession, whether they are collectively renamed a community legal service or not. To meet the declining sums of money allocated from the turn of the century, overall legal aid funding of solicitors and barristers will begin to decline. This, by itself and whatever is the technical method of implementation, will have dramatic effects in what has been the legal profession's big secret. The economy may, or may not, have been booming: legal aid certainly has. The expansion of legal aid practitioners, a feature of the growth of both branches of the legal profession over the last 20 years, will be brought to an abrupt halt.

An administrative agenda is not only driving developments in legal aid: it is also apparent in relation to civil justice. The very first recommendation of Lord Woolf's interim report was that:

> There should be a fundamental transfer in the responsibility for management of civil litigation from litigants and their legal advisers to the courts.[10]

Given the objectives of reducing 'cost, complexity and delay', Lord Woolf's basic approach was for more administrative control by the court of the pace and nature of litigation. He proposed a procedural triage: an enlarged small claims jurisdiction; a 'fast-track' for cases under £10,000 in value; and a multi-track for the most complex cases. In taking this approach, he was greatly influenced by developments in

North America where 'case management', greater administrative control of litigation by the judiciary, has been seized upon as one of the solutions to civil courts overloaded with slow-moving litigation. The fate of Lord Woolf's recommendations rest on their financial implications. In principle, one would expect a shift of administrative control to the court to be accompanied by a shift of cost. The adversarial system does lead to relatively low costs for courts and relatively high costs for lawyers as compared with civil law systems where the court plays more of the active role envisaged by Lord Woolf. For example, in his interim report Lord Woolf quotes figures for German costs which indicate that for a claim of the equivalent of just under £1m, the cost of the court fee is only a shade under that of the approved fee for the lawyer.[11] Civil justice policy is discussed further in Chapter 9.

The practitioner agenda

A considerable, and growing, number of practitioners derive a living from legal aid and publicly funded advice. Its preservation or extension gives practitioners a very obvious agenda. This does not mean that practitioners, or their representatives, necessarily act in any improper way but it does mean that they have a very real, material interest. Legal aid is an important source of income for both branches of the legal profession. It is becoming significant for law centres and the advice sector, both of which are already dependent on grant income from public sources for their non-legally aided work.

The dependence of barristers on legal aid remains particularly high, if somewhat concealed by the Bar's reticence to disclose its collective turnover. Legal aid still appears to provide around 30 per cent of the total income of the Bar (it was, on the Bar's own admission, 27 per cent in 1989).[12] In 1995/96, the Bar received £134m from the Legal Aid Board.[13] A further £170m or so seems to have been paid for Crown Court advocacy,[14] making a total of around £300m. The vast majority of barristers receive some payment from the Legal Aid Board every year and most spend some time in their career during which they are almost totally dependent upon it for their income. The Legal Aid Board consistently reveals statistics which show that it pays more barristers than are practising. This phenomenon is presumably due more to a statistical anomaly caused by barristers leaving practice before being paid than fraud. Nevertheless, it underlines the Bar's widespread involvement. The Board paid 8,588 barristers in 1994/95, during which time only 8,498 were in practice.[15] Senior barristers can

make considerable incomes. In 1995/96, 20 barristers received over
£140,000 from the Legal Aid Fund and nine more than £350,000 for
work in the Crown Court.[16]

Law Society figures suggest that for solicitors legal aid is about half
as important to overall turnover as for barristers, representing 14.5
per cent of total turnover in 1993–94.[17] This statistic is subject to
some methodological objection but is probably roughly right.[18] The
proportion of legal aid income for solicitors' firms outside the very
large commercial ones is, of course, even higher. Legal aid contributes
a quarter of the income of firms with under 26 partners.[19] Not only is
the proportion of solicitors' income from legal aid high, it has been
rising fast in recent years.

TABLE 5: PROPORTION OF SOLICITORS' GROSS INCOME PAID BY LEGAL AID

Year	Legal aid payments £	Gross fees £	Legal aid as percentage of gross fees
1988–89	430.3m	4,455m	9.7
1993–94	963.3m	6,622m	14.5

Legal aid is very widely distributed among both solicitors and barristers. The Law Society records that '80 per cent of all solicitors'
offices received at least one payment for legal aid work in 1994–95'.[20]
However, the figures show the emergence of an elite group of legal aid
firms that undertake most of the work. In 1996–97, 20 per cent of
offices (some 2,191) received 69 per cent of all payments (around
£770m); the previous year, the top 20 earned more than £1.7m a year
from the Legal Aid Board and a further five firms received more than
£1m in relation to criminal legal aid in the Crown Court.[21]

The first effect of a squeeze on solicitors' legal aid incomes would,
presumably, be to encourage them to maximise their possibilities of
undertaking advocacy. Around a third of the Bar's legal aid income is
vulnerable because unprotected by any monopoly rights of audience.
Those with rights of audience in the higher courts can already challenge the Bar in its once-protected monopolies. There are now over
400 solicitors with higher court advocacy rights, though many work
within the commercial sector. One of the ways in which this conflict is

currently mediated is in the dispute about whether costs for legal aid or civil cases can be calculated as one lump sum or whether advocacy should be separately accounted for. The latter does not guarantee that advocacy work would go to barristers but it does prevent solicitors emerging as fundholders of costs or legal aid and treating counsel as fundholding general practitioners can treat medical consultants, to be hired or not on their decision. Lord Mackay's white paper planned to give solicitors such powers: Lord Woolf, in his review of civil justice, did not. Indeed, in his discussion of fees under his proposals for a fast-track procedure, he reveals the extent of lobbying for a continuation of something akin to the current brief fee:

> The Bar has suggested, and I strongly agree, that [the advocacy fee] should be [payable] regardless of the length of the hearing. It will be payable whether the advocate is a solicitor or barrister.[22]

The Bar's determination to present its best case leads it to seek unusual allies. It has made great play of a scheme by which barristers will take referrals from lay advice agencies such as the CAB service. For this, it claims a number of justifications, one being that the agencies will have no need to employ solicitors, there being thereby:

> ... less burden on the public purse than increasing the number of salaried lawyers needed to give specialist advice in CABx.[23]

The practicalities of this scheme, particularly how payment of the barristers involved can be made, remain somewhat in doubt but its development has undoubtedly been a publicity coup for the Bar.

Overall, solicitors are probably in worse financial shape than barristers. Their conveyancing monopoly was breached in the late 1980s. The Conservative government's competition agenda provided a rollercoaster ride as, on one flank, the Law Society waged battle against the banks and financial institutions to protect conveyancing and, on another, fought the Bar for rights of audience in the higher courts. The advent of advertising and the sustained downturn in the residential property market hit the high street practitioner hard. The annual number of residential transactions virtually halved between 1988 and 1995, though it may be on the rise again. Advertising has severely reduced the profit per conveyance. The result has been the increased instability of the smaller firm, traditionally dependent on this form of income. In these circumstances, the development of legal aid as a major source of alternative income has been a godsend.

Thus, the Law Society has remained a major force in the politics of legal aid, playing a hand of varying degrees of sophistication over time. From the appointment of John Hayes as Secretary-General in early 1987, its administration was led for almost a decade by a liberal and shrewd team. The Society played a clever hand in response to the 1986 Efficiency Scrutiny, buying itself links with the voluntary sector. The Society's administration also walked a careful, and broadly successful, course as its members became increasingly shrill on the subject of legal aid remuneration, reaching a peak when west country solicitors withdrew their labour from the police station duty solicitor scheme in the early 1990s. This was particularly difficult for the Society because it was acutely aware of the difference of perception between its members and the public or the Lord Chancellor on fee income, which was in fact rising sharply overall at the time.

The Law Society's particular strength is more in the media than in Parliament, where barristers tend to dominate. Its position on legal aid has remained relatively constant throughout the past turbulent times. It has, with a relatively high degree of comfort, combined defence of its members' interest in legal aid with the role of enlightened defender of the rights of the poor. For example, the Society has had a creditable record in defending the right of silence and the rights of suspects. Its evidence to the Royal Commission on Criminal Justice was liberal on these civil rights issues. The Society has even remained relatively restrained about the increased role for advice agencies in legal aid, evidently taking the view that overt hostility would be counterproductive: it has, however, avoided the fulsome support given by the Bar. As spending becomes tighter, the Society's dual role as defender of the poor and of its members will become more difficult. Tensions within the solicitors' profession have been given a political dimension in terms of opening up competition between its relatively liberal establishment and its challengers who favour shifting the balance more to professional than public interest. As a result, the Society's council and its presidential elections have recently tended to reflect the conflict between its protectionist and liberal forces.

A major extension of legal aid funding to the voluntary sector would provide another difficult challenge for the Law Society. The financial temptation for the advice sector in general, and the CAB service in particular, is clear. Its national office currently works on a £16m budget, three-quarters of which comes from the Department of Trade and Industry: bureaux receive around £43m from local authorities.[24] The service is, undoubtedly, stretched to its financial limits. In these circumstances, sums of money such as the £11m spent annually on housing green form advice become an understandable temptation. The problem for the CAB service and other advice agencies is the extent to which it can deliver services of a comparable level to solicitors. This is an almost unanswerable question since little research on this topic exists. A research project has now been devised to test this and its results should be carefully considered: it is a critical issue.

Two other issues arise for the advice sector in the push for legal aid finance: the extent to which its internal organisation can match the profit-oriented management of legal aid firms and the degree to which its own networks can hold together agencies within and outside the legal aid scheme. The latter is a potential problem more for the CAB service than other, looser, groupings such as the Federation of Independent Advice Centres. Participation in legal aid will certainly extend the professionalism of voluntary agencies. It will increase the already existing trend to employ specialist workers and raise issues about the role of volunteer advisers in the provision of a statutory service. This raises particular difficulties for the CAB network because of its hard-won battle for unified and national standards of performance. In time, the not-for-profit sector may well be driven to some form of restructuring in which a common identity of interest and organisation is developed between agencies participating in legal aid, ie, the advice agencies with legal aid contracts and law centres, and those outside.

There are other relevant agendas in the civil justice field, in particular one that might be designated as judicial. Judges have a considerable interest in how their courts work; they can be swayed by access to justice considerations, as was Mr Justice Laws; they can also be said to have an almost collective administrative law agenda in terms of broad advocacy, though differing detail, of a developing role for judicial review. The next chapters focus, however, on the potential interplay between the policies of the new Labour government with the administrative and practitioner agendas discussed above.

REFERENCES

1 *Hansard HL Debates*, 15 December 1987, col 606.
2 Ibid, col 607.
3 Ibid, col 608.
4 Legal Aid Board *Response to the Lord Chancellor's Consultation Paper* (Legal Aid Board, 1995).
5 G Bull and J Steele *Legal Aid Franchising for Non-solicitor Agencies: interim report* (Policy Studies Institute, 1995), p7.

6 J Steele and G Bull *Fast, Friendly and Expert? Legal Aid Franchising in Advice Agencies without Solicitors* (Policy Studies Institute, 1996), p125.

7 See, eg, 'Transaction Criteria: the face of the future' February 1993 *Legal Action* 9.

8 Cm 3305 (HMSO, 1996).

9 Lord Irvine of Lairg QC, Speech to the Bar Conference, 28 September 1996.

10 Repeated as recommendation 1, Lord Woolf *Access to Justice: Final Report* (HMSO, 1996).

11 Lord Woolf, *Access to Justice: Interim Report* (HMSO, 1995), Annex V, p263.

12 Bar Council Strategy Group *Strategies for the Future* (1989), p18.

13 Legal Aid Board *Annual Report 1995–96* (HMSO, 1996), p105.

14 *Judicial Review Statistics 1995,* table 10.7 shows Crown Court payments at a total of £309m for 1995 and Law Society *Annual Statistical Report 1996* indicates that £133m was paid to solicitors in 1995–96.

15 Legal Aid Board *Annual Report 1995–96* (HMSO) and General Council of the Bar *Annual Report 1995.*

16 Letter from Garry Streeter MP to Frank Field MP, dated February 1997 (sic). These figures are admittedly for receipts and this might, for some recipients, include payments for more than one year.

17 Law Society *Annual Statistical Report 1995*, p63.

18 It includes disbursements and VAT but excludes payments from legally aided clients and their opponents.

19 Law Society (n17), para 7.10.

20 Ibid, p59.

21 Legal Aid Board *Annual Report 1996–97* (HMSO) and letter to Frank Field MP (see n16).

22 Lord Woolf *Access to Justice: Final Report* (HMSO, 1996), p52.

23 Bar Council *Partners for Access to Justice; Legal Services under Labour* (1996), p5.

24 NACAB *Annual Report 1995/96.*

CHAPTER 4

Labour: the new government's agenda

> New Labour is the political arm of none other than the British people as
> a whole. Our values are the same: the equal worth of all, with no one
> cast aside; fairness and justice within strong communities.
>
> New Labour *Because Britain Deserves Better* (1997 Manifesto), p2.

With such expansive promises, Labour won a landslide victory on
1 May 1997, ending up with a majority of 179 over its largest rival.
Eighteen years of Conservative government came to a decisive end.
Labour ministers stepped into power with the lightest of political
burdens imposed upon them as manifesto commitments, outside
certain core pledges. Thus, in relation to legal services, Lord Irvine
was directed only as follows:

> Labour will undertake a wide-ranging review both of the reform of the
> civil justice system and Legal Aid. We will achieve value for money for
> the taxpayer and the consumer. A community legal service will develop
> local, regional and national plans for the development of Legal Aid
> according to the needs and priorities of regions and areas. The key to
> success will be to promote a partnership between the voluntary sector,
> the legal profession and the Legal Aid Board.[1]

As was common throughout the 1997 manifesto, content was
somewhat less detailed than in 1992. This would have committed a
government under Neil Kinnock to:

> . . . improve access to legal aid and, when resources allow, extend it to
> tribunal hearings. We will encourage the expansion of voluntary advice
> centres and invest in better support for victims. We will appoint from the
> House of Commons a Minister for Legal Administration, who will
> initially be part of the Lord Chancellor's Department. We will go on to
> create a Department of Legal Administration headed by a Minister in the

Commons who will be responsible for all courts and tribunals in England and Wales.[2]

Thus, an emphasis on institutional reform had been reduced to the idea of developing legal aid into a community legal service, with the details uncharted.

A major general difference between the two manifestos was the greater attention to financial prudence given in 1997 as compared with five years earlier. Gordon Brown's commitment to live within Conservative government estimates for the first two years of government has already been noted. Following such caution, no commitment was made in 1997 to improve legal aid even 'when resources allow'. The announcement that Sir Peter Middleton was to head the combined review of legal aid and civil justice underlined the toughness presented in relation to financial prudence.

In consequence, it is absolutely clear that an aspiration to improve legal services through greater expenditure will remain an aspiration. The Labour government accepts the need to contain public expenditure and, hence, may be driven by a very similar administrative agenda as its predecessor, in order to do it. A different approach is, however, possible. The following chapters indicate that there is an alternative, even in relation to how costs can be controlled. This does not involve resorting to capping expenditure and introducing compulsory competitive tendering, the essential basis of Lord Mackay's approach.

The new element in the 1997 manifesto was the mention of a 'community legal service'. This is an idea which first surfaced in Labour's policy document, entitled in full *Access to Justice: Labour's proposals for reforming the civil justice system*, and passed by almost universal acclaim at its 1995 annual conference. Among the few dissenters were veteran left-winger Tony Benn and maverick Austin Mitchell who felt that the document should have contained a commitment to introduce a national salaried legal service. Labour's document, still referred to as an authoritative source of policy on Labour's website, set out its wares under four headings:

First, our aim must be to maximise access to justice . . .

Second, we need to empower our citizens by ensuring that people know what their legal rights and responsibilities are and are clear about how to assert those rights and enforce the responsibilities of others to them . . .

Third, we must make the best possible use of public and private resources available for legal services . . .

Fourth, the justice system must be seen to work for all citizens, not just a privileged few, and must command public confidence.[3]

These are broad objectives to which it is difficult to conceive much opposition from any political quarter. Some of the document's policies were effectively bipartisan and followed Lord Mackay's approach for the Conservative government. For example, Labour espoused ADR where appropriate, in particular in relation to family mediation.

There were some differences. Labour wanted to hive off judicial appointment to a separate commission, an idea supported by Lord Irvine in an important pre-election speech to the Bar annual conference in the autumn of 1996. Labour wanted to place a new emphasis on public legal education, an idea espoused in places like Australia, Canada and the USA but largely foreign to this country:

A just society depends on people knowing their rights and responsibilities.

We intend to encourage the promotion of public legal education and awareness of the rights and responsibilities of citizenship through all schools, advice centres, libraries and courtrooms.[4]

Labour's 'big idea' is the argument for a community legal service to replace legal aid. The precise meaning seems still to be open to discussion and has been taken as the basis for presenting the policy set out in later chapters. In a speech to the House of Lords in the summer of 1997, Lord Irvine apparently sought to limit the idea to the advice component of legal aid:

We have a Manifesto commitment to develop, not abolish community legal services. A high priority therefore attaches to the £151 million which they currently cost.[5]

The original idea was broader and implied at the very least a greater coherence of service provision than has hitherto existed. *Access to Justice* was at pains to explain:

We are not intending to establish a salaried public legal service, but one in which a range of services is offered by independent providers. The franchising system will be improved and used to monitor and maintain high standards of service delivery and value for money.[6]

More radical developments might be expected in the future:

We do, however, envisage that over time the community legal service will expand its employment of salaried lawyers with rights of audience in the courts so as to provide high quality, affordable representation at lower cost to the taxpayer than the existing system.[7]

The community legal service might also develop so that its clientele extended to:

> ... private clients at an appropriate charge, as well as publicly funded clients.

Access to Justice retained a commitment, similar to that in Lord Mackay's approach, to local planning through regional legal services committees. However, the mechanism would clearly be different. Lord Irvine, speaking after publication of Lord Mackay's white paper published in the summer of 1996, took clear issue with his predecessor's cost-capping approach. This was:

> ... unattractive in principle, because legal aid would cease to be a benefit to which a qualifying individual is entitled. It would in practice become a discretionary benefit ... [8]

His view at that time was that:

> The Legal Aid Budget is currently within estimate and under broad control so there is no immediate imperative for cost-capping.

The Middleton review

For Lord Irvine, cost is clearly a major concern, both in relation to legal aid and the proposals of Lord Woolf. Hence, the announcement of Sir Peter Middleton's review. Its terms of reference are worth quoting in full:

> 1. To conduct a review of civil justice and legal aid to consider whether existing proposals for reform are the right way to deliver the following objectives:
> (a) to reduce the cost, delay and complexity of civil litigation; and
> (b) to gain better control of the cost of legal aid, better value for money for the resources available, and the ability to target those resources on the areas of greatest need.
> 2. To make recommendations on whether the current proposals are workable, whether they are likely to be cost-effective, what the priorities should be for their implementation (where appropriate), and whether there are alternative approaches that ought to be examined further.
> 3. In particular, the review is to consider:
> (a) whether the civil justice reforms can be implemented without imposing costs which outweigh savings both for potential litigants and the courts;

(b) the means by which the cost of legal aid can be kept within limits which society can afford and is willing to pay in the context of the overall public expenditure ceilings to which the Government is committed, while giving the fullest possible weight to the important values of legal aid as a rights-based entitlement equally available throughout the country;

(c) the interaction between the two reform programmes, including the costs/benefits of civil justice reforms to the legal aid fund, and the extent to which legal aid systems can re-inforce the objectives of the civil justice reforms;

(d) how far relevant aspects of the reforms (for example involving the not-for-profit sector, information services, use of ADR) might be developed to lay the foundations for a Community Legal Service.

The review is expected to produce an interim report at the end of September 1997 and a final report by the end of the year. Its recommendations can, thus, be measured against those of this book: how legal aid costs can be controlled; how a community legal service might be established; how legal aid might be developed; how reform of civil procedure might be integrated with that of legal aid.

REFERENCES

1 New Labour *Because Britain Deserves Better* (1997 Manifesto), to be found at http://www.labour.org.uk.
2 Labour *It's Time to Get Britain Working Again* (1992 Manifesto), p24.
3 *Access to Justice* (1995), p3.
4 Ibid, p7.
5 Speech, 14 July 1997.
6 *Access to Justice* (1995), p4.
7 Ibid.
8 Speech, 28 September 1996.

CHAPTER 5

Legal aid: how to live within a budget

Public finances must be sustainable over the long term.
Rt Hon Gordon Brown MP, Budget Speech, 2 July 1997.

Lord Mackay laid out Conservative plans for bringing legal aid within budget in a fivefold plan in his 1996 white paper. These involved:

> ... replacing the present open-ended approach to resources with pre-determined budgets that can be allocated to meet local demand within national priorities; extending the scheme to new types of providers and services; introducing contracts between providers of services and the Legal Aid Board for specified services of defined quality at an agreed price; a new test for deciding whether civil cases should be given legal aid. This will target available resources on the most deserving cases; and changing the rules governing financial conditions to increase the potential liability of assisted persons to contribute to their own and, in civil cases, their opponents' costs.[1]

This is certainly a package that would have contained costs. However, the same objective can be achieved by better means.

An alternative approach is desirable because strict cash-limiting, the institution of what might be called a 'hard cap' to expenditure, necessarily involves rationing. A set sum of money is made available and the service provided becomes supply- rather than demand-led. The retention of any absolute and overriding rights to service by potential clients becomes difficult. Hence, the Conservative government linked the hard cap with a system of prioritisation or rationing as a way of ensuring that demand was manipulated to meet supply. Lord Irvine noted the ensuing problems in his speech to the Bar conference. Legal aid would become:

... a benefit which would have to be disallowed when the money ran out, or when another category of case was given preference. Legal aid would cease to be a service available on an equal basis nationally, because cases would go forward in one region where identical cases in others, of equal merit, would not.[2]

Nevertheless, any alternative mechanism has to meet some difficult goals. Assuming that legal aid will be no exception to the general containment of expenditure within Conservative estimates, then Lord Irvine has to deliver it within the following limits:[3]

TABLE 6: CONSERVATIVE GOVERNMENT ESTIMATES ON LEGAL AID EXPENDITURE

1996/97	1997/98	1998/99	1999/00
£	£	£	£
1,477m	1,561m	1,602m	1,518m

Thus, predicted expenditure contracts in the millennium year. At a point, it is obvious that a reduction of government expenditure must entail a reduction in services. For nearly two decades, much political debate has denied this obvious fact and the fiction has been maintained of a holy grail wherein improved services and reduced expenditure can be harmoniously stirred. An adequate access to justice policy that implemented the ten principles enunciated in Chapter 1 would require additional expenditure. So too would any major expansion of state-funded services, from health to education. Contemporary practical politics require, however, recognition that this is not a convincing message for politicians wrestling with a sceptical electorate. This book, therefore, proceeds on the basis of an acceptance that, in practice, funding will be limited. As the political situation develops and changes, it may be that tax and spend policies come more into fashion, as they might if the issue of social exclusion and division is given greater priority. This would certainly allow more to be done in the field of legal services and access to justice. In the meantime, the most practical hope is that governments will become more disposed to allocate new funding for new projects which offer measurable success in terms of attaining new goals. This book contains plenty of examples of what might be funded in such circumstances.

From hard cap to soft cap

Legal aid has been demand-led in the manner of social security income payments and not cash-limited like the Social Fund or healthcare. There is a danger that Lord Mackay's draconian response will become new orthodoxy. Cash-limiting would require legislation to change the basis of the scheme and, before this is introduced, it is desirable to reconsider these proposals with care.

The pressures on expenditure are clear. The demand-led system has allowed practitioners a desirable flexibility to the demands of their clients but has also channelled responses within certain categories. No overall planning has been possible. As a consequence, lawyers in private practice have responded differently to different needs. For example, solicitors sharply recognised the previously ignored demands of battered women from the late 1970s onward. This was, no doubt, partly as the result of campaigning work by women's organisations and law centres. It was also undoubtedly motivated by the withdrawal of legal aid for undefended divorce which took place at about the same time. They have been slower to respond to demand in less traditional areas such as social welfare law (eg, consumer, welfare benefits, employment, immigration and housing). For all of the late run on green form, it can still prove hard to obtain an expert solicitor in these areas, particularly outside the larger cities. Solicitors have been unable to meet certain needs through the continued lack of funding, most notably those of families faced with coroners' inquests or tribunal applicants where legal aid has remained largely unavailable. It is, therefore, reasonable to search for ways which can control, and for some types of work even direct, the growth of expenditure without providing a hard cap that gives rise to arbitrary decisions at the level of the individual client.

A 'soft cap', ie, the limitation of expenditure within estimate as in any business budgeting process, requires three elements of accurate prediction:

- the cost per legal aid case;
- the number of cases;
- the duration of cases.

The Lord Chancellor's Department has historically proved somewhat inadequate in its prediction of these variables, though it is becoming much more accurate. Control of the cost per case should become easier with the increased use of fixed fees; improved computerisation of Legal Aid Board records and the improved management represented by the Board. Fixed fees need not extend to all cases, only a sufficient number to allow accurate prediction of the total budget for each type of case, particularly if attention is paid to high cost cases. As to the number of cases, the overall figures are so high and trends relatively foreseeable that it should be possible to predict expenditure with some accuracy. The fact that cases begin, and are identified as beginning by way of the issue of legal aid certificates, well before they are paid means that a handle can be gained on cost. If the number of cases in one year is known to have risen, eg, with a surge of expensive medical negligence cases, then cost can be managed by cuts to remuneration or coverage in the next. Given the size and complexity of the legal aid budget, a relatively accurate match between prediction and outturn should be achievable. If not, the first approach should be to improve the procedures of government. Unless this fails, the answer cannot be simply to shift the burden of rationing to the level of the individual supplier of services. This may be tempting for administrators, whether civil servants or politicians, but it is not fundamentally responsible or good government.

Some flexibility could be obtained by setting the budget for a rolling three-year forward period. Any overrun in one year would be corrected in the next. This would allow an element of flexibility if it was required and acceptable. In addition and if absolutely necessary to persuade the Treasury of rigid financial probity, the option could be retained to deal with serious overruns by holding back payment from one year to the next so that corrective action could be taken. This would provide a fallback mechanism by which the sceptical could be assured that a soft cap could, if required, become every bit as rigid as a hard cap. A competent standard of administration and management by the Board and LCD officials should, however, avoid the use of such a mechanism. Operation of the budgeting process is a fundamental component of the greater attention which should be given to the planning of provision. This is discussed in the next chapter (see p62).

A specific issue arises as to whether the position in relation to legal advice is any different to that of legal aid as a whole. Lord Irvine has implied that it might be:

> . . . the overriding question in our review will be whether block contracts for advice and assistance but not civil litigation together with effective control over . . . high costs cases . . . would be enough without a system of block contracts for litigation.[4]

Departmental estimates show legal advice as, in effect, already capped at the 1996–97 level for the next three years (see TABLE 7).

TABLE 7: ESTIMATED EXPENDITURE ON LEGAL ADVICE[5]

1996–97	1997–98	1998–99	1999–00
£m	£m	£m	£m
274	266	280	275

Reduction of the unit price

In principle, the capping of advice suffers from the same problems as the capping of aid. If expenditure is to be limited, then there should be a search for ways of retaining payment by reference to units of work undertaken. The Legal Aid Board is currently researching the effect of different payment mechanisms with solicitors. However, just as for legal aid, the first way of making savings and keeping within a soft cap should be to look at ways of reducing the unit price of advice. What is required is the pinpoint targeting of savings which are identified by ruthless attention to detail and the scanning of information available to, or obtainable by, the Legal Aid Board about how legal aid and advice is working in practice. Criminal legal advice provides a good example. Some practitioners have undoubtedly increased claims for green form advice on criminal matters to compensate for the introduction of fixed fees. That was contrary to their spirit and could be stopped by the introduction of a regulation against such 'double dipping'. That would preserve criminal legal advice in myriad other situations where it is desirable. Welfare benefits provide another example. Advice under this heading now accounts for 165,000 bills a year at an average cost of £78 each. This is a total of £13m a year. It is highly likely that a considerable amount is dispersed on simple benefit assessment and checking. If this is so, the issue should be addressed by limiting the amount claimable for such advice and encouraging appropriate referral.

Somehow, whether a soft or a hard cap is adopted, the unit price of legal aid cases has to fall. Demand is rising; expectation is rising; eligibility for both legal aid and advice is so low that too many people are falling into the justice trap of being too poor to pay privately but too well off to receive legal aid. This is particularly the case in areas, such as violence against women by their partners, where there is no possibility of insurance, pre or post the event, or of using conditional fees.

The Conservative government's response to this issue was the introduction of what was, in effect, compulsory competitive tendering by legal aid practitioners for blocks of work. This is, however, a particularly blunt weapon with a number of major disadvantages; it is competitive only until the point the contract is granted, thereafter it is not competitive at all; it requires an omniscient bureaucracy to administer the bidding process; it is necessarily a system that is slow to respond to new needs and changing demands because contracts will be awarded on the basis of need as perceived at the point of the contract; block contracts for a finite sum of money would be either for a finite sum of cases, leading potentially to unmet need and encouraging cherry-picking of the easiest type of cases and client, or for an infinite number of cases, in which case the supplier will be tempted to minimise their number and quality.

A new approach is required. The unit price can be reduced in a number of ways.

First, high cost cases in general should be examined to see what savings might be made. These take up a disproportionate amount of legal aid expenditure. For example, as Lord Irvine told the Bar Conference:

> ... 46 per cent of the criminal legal aid budget for higher Court cases goes on a mere 1 per cent of the cases. That 1 per cent accounts for well over £100m.
> In the civil legal aid scheme 1 per cent of the cases takes 15 per cent of the budget.

This raises, though is not limited to, the issue of the high rate of QCs' fees (see p39). The earnings of those in the civil field look particularly questionable. A mere 10 per cent reduction in earnings of 13 leading counsel would apparently lead to a saving of nearly £400,000 a year. Nine of them would still have earned close to, or over, one-third of a million pounds. These sorts of incomes are not sustainable given the impact on clients of cuts to their eligibility and the weight of contributions which they are now expected to pay. This cannot, however, be done in isolation from QCs' incomes from the public purse more generally. If this is to be prioritised for legal aid then, logically, the Crown Prosecution Service and the government generally have to come to a common policy over payment: it would be manifestly inequitable to encourage a situation where leading counsel appearing for the Crown obtained higher payment that one appearing for the defence. What is necessary is a research-based analysis of Legal Aid Board data on the reasons for high cost and a pragmatic approach to reducing expenditure.

Second, particular action could be taken in relation to multi-party actions by adopting the Board's latest proposals. This would recognise that such cases are often more akin to class actions than a true aggregation of individual claims. As a result, more artificiality might be tolerated in relation to their costs than otherwise because the cases are more constructed by lawyers. In consequence, it might be permissible to reduce the costs payable by the Board in the event of failure, in the knowledge that solicitors stand to make large sums in the event of success. This would not, however, seem appropriate for other civil or criminal cases simply because they are large cases. There is no reason why costs should not be paid on the usual basis.

Third, there may be scope for pinpoint targeting of potential cuts, as for legal advice. Hitherto, the approach to cuts has been too broadbrush. Specific examination is required of the explosion of representation in relation to children generally and under the Children Act. The Legal Aid Board now receives over 100,000 applications for legal aid under the Children Act, of which it grants just under 90 per cent. Merits are not tested in public law proceedings which account for just under 20,000 legal aid certificates in this area. Per case, High Court Children Act proceedings are higher both in average solicitor and counsel costs than any other type of case.[6] Much of this may be, and undoubtedly is, justified. Nevertheless, there are cases where representation does appear to go to excess and these should be reviewed to see if any lessons can be drawn. This is the sort of precise examination of individual types of cases that is required to make a proper impact on 'per case' expenditure.

Fourth, the Legal Aid Board should develop franchising in the way that was originally intended. This was as a partnership with 'preferred suppliers' who would improve their management, reduce their costs and provide better services. This 'win-win' dream is still possible. The future of legal aid lies, certainly within urban areas, with the large battalions which should be able to run more economically than smaller units. At this stage, force is probably not even required. A degree of volume could be inserted into the contractual provisions of legal aid franchises. Once an acceptable degree of coverage across the country had been obtained, unfranchised practitioners could be placed under restrictions as to the circumstances in which they could claim legal aid, eg, to build up to obtain a franchise or because of previous contact with a client.

The value of building a partnership with providers was demonstrated by Lord Woolf. Considerable numbers of lawyers assisted his thinking in how to simplify procedures and, in doing so, worked against what might have been regarded as their short-term material interests. His object, after all, was to reduce costs. The best group able to identify these cases, and to bring down costs generally, are the practitioners concerned. Now is a particularly ripe time to build a partnership with them. Many recognise that their long-term self-interest lies in a stable and protected legal aid budget. Accordingly, it may well be possible to get the sort of partnership in terms of legal aid that Lord Woolf obtained in relation to civil justice reform. This kind of approach might be seen as insufficiently aggressive in presentational terms: the imposition of a hard cap and accompanying howls of protest might seem temptingly to be doing more about the problem. We are, however, now at a unique position in relation to legal aid. Practitioners can read the practical politics and they have been softened up by Lord Mackay's decade-long war of attrition. The best of them should be deployed as allies rather than pushed into a position of hostility.

An important element of defence for the practitioner would be to maintain payment of some kind per case rather than accepting bulk payment for infinite amounts of work. The way forward is to follow a pragmatic combination of standard fees and encouragement of legal aid practitioners to provide more services in bulk and by specialists: the statistics reveal legal aid very much still to be a cottage industry where savings should be possible by speeding up the administration of cases without harming the service to clients. Considerable advances should be possible which allow both control of the budget and the fostering of a group of practitioners who are specialist, larger providers who see themselves as working with their funder to a common end rather than against it. Furthermore, the most self-enlightened practitioners recognise that the long-term defence of legal aid as a source of public expenditure and private income depends upon its perception as politically desirable and broadly available.

Finally, some types of case might be differently funded. An example, consistently promoted by LAG though largely greeted by silence, has been the very high cost criminal cases that relate to serious fraud. Many of these cases constitute a distinct group. They concern allegations of dishonesty in complex financial transactions involving large amounts of money by defendants who were, at the time, extremely well off. The ultimate sanction in a legal aid case, withdrawal of legal representation, is not effective. The prosecution, the court and the defence has an interest in effective legal representation. A consultation document from the Lord Chancellor's Department and others, published in 1992, suggested that in such cases defendants might be required to have representation:

> The Government is aware of the difficulties involved in obliging a defendant to accept a lawyer he has not chosen. Defendants do not, however, have an unfettered right to conduct their own defence in the manner they choose ... It is therefore suggested that the court should have the power to appoint an *amicus curiae* to represent an unrepresented defendant.[7]

It is clear, therefore, that eligibility rules in serious fraud cases that exclude too many defendants might be self-defeating from the point of view of the interests of justice.

As a result, it might be better to see these cases as part of the unavoidable cost of regulation of the City of London and the complex financial dealings that it represents. Commercial interests require these cases to be brought in order to preserve their integrity and London's international reputation as an honest centre of business. Hence, it too has an interest in the successful determination of such cases. Accordingly, consideration should be given as to whether the defence of all cases of serious fraud involving defined aspects of financial services and transactions should be paid out of a special fund. The resources of the fund would not come from the taxpayer but from the City's regulatory bodies. They would be reimbursed through subscription by those whom they regulate. The costs would, thus, fall upon those with the closest interest in the issues under investigation. This would have the advantage of providing an incentive for both regulators and the bulk of those regulated to stamp out fraud. There seems little reason why the cost of regulation of the City of London should fall upon the general taxpayer.

A more often considered alternative is the potential role for conditional or contingency fees. Conditional fees have been permitted by the Courts and Legal Services Act 1990 in personal injury cases on the basis that lawyers may take a case at no fee to their clients but receive double their usual costs if they win, subject to consent of the court and a Law Society-advised maximum of 25 per cent of the total money sum awarded to the client. The arrangement is often described as 'no win, no fee' in the media though it is hardly that in practice because clients are not protected by the conditional fee arrangement from the potential award of costs in favour of their opponent if they lose. This requires the purchase of an insurance policy, the premium for which currently costs a little under £90.

Conditional fee arrangements have certainly proved popular with personal injury lawyers. Over 12,000 have been made to date. Preliminary research is about to be published on how these fees have operated in practice though the results will be coloured by the fact that so few cases have yet had time to proceed through the system if they were not settled at a relatively early stage. Conditional fees represent a temptation to a hard pressed government to regard them as an alternative to legal aid. There are problems, however. First, personal injury cases have such a high success rate that the savings of cutting them out from legal aid cover would be very small, apparently around £20m a year. More relevant would be the administrative savings for the Legal Aid Board because personal injury cases amount to around a half of all civil, non-matrimonial certificates. Most cases are withdrawn from legal aid just before settlement so that the client's liability is covered during the period of doubt and the solicitor can receive a higher rate of payment in costs once the case has been resolved. Therefore, a better second point is simply to impose a charge on a solicitor who wishes to take this course of action sufficient to cover the administrative expenses of processing the case to date. Third, the cost savings would be speculative since it would be manifestly unfair to require clients who are currently on legal aid to pay the cost of the insurance premium, at least where this would be more than would be payable by way of legal aid contributions. Fourth, the extent to which conditional fees could be extended beyond personal injuries remains in doubt. It would surely, for example, be politically controversial to extend them to defamation or maintenance cases. Fifth, conditional fees eat into damages which have been purportedly assessed by scientific measures. For a client whose case is such that conditional fees are capped at the 25 per cent level of damages, such fees are indistinguishable in fact from a contingency fee arrangement of the same amount. Two dangers follow. Judges might raise damages to compensate for the element that they know will be diverted to lawyers, as apparently happens in the United States among juries, and/or the whole estimating process for damages will be thrown into disrepute because everyone concerned knows that what the litigant will receive has become essentially arbitrary.

Some caution is, thus, required. More research is needed on how exactly they operate before policy decisions can be safely taken. It may well be that they do benefit some classes of litigants but, particularly if legal aid is withdrawn on the basis that they represent a satisfactory alternative, they may disadvantage others. Winners are likely to be people with straightforward cases, high damages at stake and high incomes, above legal aid limits: conditional fees may help them take litigation that is otherwise too dangerous in terms of the potential liability for costs. Losers may be people with less certain cases of lower amounts and on lower incomes whom legal aid might have assisted. Their interests could be protected to some extent if the lawyer was required to advance the insurance premium, not perhaps unreasonable in terms of the potentially double remuneration at stake.

An objective test of merits

The imposition of a soft cap has the enormous merit of allowing the retention of a rights-based model of entitlement on an objective basis. The example of the Social Fund shows the problems of moving to some form of discretionary scheme. Entitlement becomes arbitrary, as reported by the Department of Social Security's own researchers:

> The needs and circumstances of unsuccessful applicants cannot be shown to be significantly different from those of successful applicants.[8]

Legal aid must retain an objective test of merit, however it is formulated.

There has been discussion of the level at which the merits test should be set for civil legal aid. The current generally applicable tests (legal aid is available in certain limited cases on a more generous basis, eg, in some cases involving children) are set out in the Legal Aid Act 1988.[9] There must be reasonable grounds for taking, defending or being a party to the proceedings and it should not be unreasonable that legal aid be granted. A continuing theme of the last few years has been the idea, promoted in parts of the media, that legal aid is available for unmeritorious cases. Such is the head of steam behind this idea that it requires some response, regardless of its truth. First, the Legal Aid Board needs to consider its own procedures. Not all questionable cases will be the result of appeals to the practitioner panels that can overrule its judgment. Second, there could be an anti-abuse provision designed to catch some of the more notorious cases. Third, any reform should await the work being done by the Legal Aid Board already to match the predictions of solicitors and barristers with outcomes to identify any systematic abuse of the scheme.

Many of the media 'horror' stories have turned out, in the event, to be false. There is a danger that any response going beyond the three steps set out above would be disproportionate. The current tests import two considerations of reasonableness. Any tightening would logically require the importing of some degree of unreasonableness. It has been suggested that the merits test could be reduced to percentage figures of success but, in practice, deciding between a case at 50/50, 60/40 or 70/30 chances of winning cannot be a scientific exercise. This is particularly so when only one side of the case is known. The real abuse may be that some barristers and solicitors unjustifiably inflate their clients' chances of success in order to obtain legal aid that would not otherwise be available. If so, this should be dealt with directly by monitoring their prediction record and questioning their competence if it deviates too much from results as they become known. In any event, a system of limited certificates combined with a requirement of continual reassessment of the chances of success should severely limit the Board's risk.

There is one respect in which the merits test should be widened. Legal Aid Board guidance currently states:

> . . . public interest . . . will rarely be a significant consideration in legal aid decisions.[10]

'Public interest' is a wide term and can clearly encompass a number of different situations. It is understandable that government might want to limit the number of cases funded by the Board on this ground, particularly as many of them would otherwise be brought against its own departments. However, if the taking of a case is genuinely in the public interest then manifestly it is against that interest that it not be taken. The potential operation of a public interest criteria should be reviewed. In the meantime, the Board's guidance should surely be amended to allow a broader account to be taken of the public interest, for example, where the point at issue is a matter of arguable statutory construction.

A community legal service

The next two chapters consider how Labour might develop its idea of a community legal service. Chapter 6 deals with its organisation; Chapter 7 with the services it might provide.

REFERENCES

1 Lord Chancellor's Department *Striking the Balance: the future of legal aid in England and Wales* Cm 3305 (HMSO, 1996), para 1.17.
2 Speech, 28 September 1996.
3 LCD Press Release, 26 November 1996.
4 Speech (see n2).
5 Lord Chancellor's and Law Officers' Departments *The Government's Expenditure Plans 1994–95 to 1996–97* Cm 2509 (HMSO, 1994), p30.
6 Legal Aid Board *Annual Report 1995–96* (HMSO, 1996), p68.
7 Lord Chancellor's Department, Home Office, Legal Secretariat to the Law Officers *Consultation Paper on Long Criminal Trials* (1992), para 3.13.
8 M Huby and G Dill *Evaluating the Social Fund* (HMSO, 1992), para 12.4.
9 See s15.
10 *Legal Aid Handbook 1996/97* (Sweet and Maxwell, 1997), p69.

CHAPTER 6

Community legal services: planning and organisation

> In place of the waste and inefficiency of the current system, we propose to create a community legal service, co-ordinated by existing regional legal aid board offices.
>
> Labour *Access to Justice* (1995), p4.

The very idea of a change of name from legal aid to a community legal service implies a greater coherence of provision. This chapter considers the mechanisms by which a community legal service might be planned, administered and organised.

Planning

There could hardly be less planning than now: the service provided in any geographical area or for any type of case is currently determined by the random decision-making of individual providers, largely firms of solicitors, within the limits of nationally set levels of eligibility and scope. Thus, the availability of legal assistance with, say, housing disrepair cases will be determined not only by the impact of eligibility rules for legal aid and the needs of prospective clients in any locality but the value given to this work by the solicitors' firms in the area. In all too many places, lawyers have historically not cared, needed or been able to provide skilled services in areas of law like landlord and tenant, for all that they have done so much more in matrimonial and personal injury cases.

A community legal service should be able to deliver better planned services through a better organised partnership of providers. Other jurisdictions provide models of how this can be done through a combination of a semi-independent body like the Legal Aid Board.

For example, in the United States, the Legal Services Corporation (LSC) receives an allocation of funds from Congress for civil legal services. It divides this into estimated expenditure for appropriate geographical areas of the country, with the sum derived from a calculation based on the number of people within a definition of poverty. This has provided a relatively equitable way of dividing up the total grant. It is, however, a mechanism with a number of drawbacks. First, provision varies around the United States as there are no universal levels of entitlement and different schemes spend their money in different ways. This is not as important an issue in such a large country, already divided into over 50 individual states with different laws and traditions, as it might be here. Second, the allocation of sums is very low and has been dropping. Its 1997 budget is only $283m for the whole USA, as compared with our £1.5bn for England and Wales alone, with a total population about one-fifth of the size. These are, therefore, on any scale, relatively marginal sums of money in terms of the legal services provided. If they were more important, the method of control might attract more controversy. Third, the high degree of centralism has perhaps encouraged political intervention, always more likely in the USA because of the different political history of publicly funded legal services. In any event, Congress's conditions on grant receipt have now become so restrictive that legal services are now being split in many states between those that receive LSC funds and others. For example, Congress prevents a LSC-funded programme from acting for anyone in relation to an abortion or who is 'a person incarcerated in a Federal, State, or local prison'.[1]

Other jurisdictions have given their equivalents of the Legal Aid Board more autonomy than the LSC has currently obtained. Some employ a model where government does little more than give a lump sum to the administrative body and then delegates decision-making to it. For example, this has been the way in which the Australian Legal Aid Commission described in *A Strategy for Justice*[2] operated. An additional element of control is given to these bodies because most of them directly employ staff. Some such organisations, like Quebec's Commission des Services Juridiques, have developed highly organised systems for controlling their employees, including an element of performance-related pay.

The Legal Aid Board set out its own recommendations for its preferred planning process in its response to Lord Mackay's green paper. This would have involved a number of stages. The Lord Chancellor would first announce allocation of resources between various budgets for crime, family and civil non-family work. The Board would then draft a provisional plan for approval by the Lord Chancellor. This would then be sent to regional legal services committees for consideration. Each committee would produce its own draft plan for its area which would then be approved by the Board and the Lord Chancellor. Contracts would then be let by the Board's area offices. The regional legal services committees would advise on how well their plans were working. Such a mechanism has desirable aspects. It involves the three relevant players: the Lord Chancellor, the Board and regional legal services committees. However, the mechanisms need to change if there is to a 'soft' cap rather than a hard one.

Any planning process has to begin with a reversal of the expenditure telescope. An overall figure for projected expenditure needs to be set and then services allocated from within it, instead of determined by it. The final plan should be published in the name of the Lord Chancellor operating on advice from the Legal Aid Board. The process should be as public as possible. The Board could be formally required to cost various options in relation to provision. The Lord Chancellor would then announce those which had been approved. Regional legal services committees might be encouraged to put forward bids for special projects for which a fund would be established. This is an idea supported by Labour's *Access to Justice*:

> In addition to providing basic legal services, each local board will be able to bid for earmarked funds from within the existing legal aid budget to establish innovative schemes to meet particular local needs.

The committees could also advise the Board on submissions that it might make on cost and need for services.

Organisation of the Legal Aid Board/Community Legal Services Authority

It is not clear whether Labour intends that the community legal service to be delivered by a new body or whether this is the new term to cover practices which are the responsibility of the existing Legal Aid Board. Certainly in the longer term, statutory reform in the shape of the creation of what this publication will term the Community Legal Services Authority (CLSA) would be desirable. This would allow reform of the existing organisation and structure. The Board has increasingly modelled itself along the lines of a commercial board of directors: three of its senior executives are now members of the Board, almost a quarter of its total composition. This creates an effective management tool and resembles the way in which legal aid administration has been reformed, including the transformation of many of the Australian Legal Aid Commissions. The Victorian commission, described in *A Strategy for Justice*,[3] has, for example, been slimmed down into Victoria Legal Aid, a body explicitly designed more for executive effectiveness than democratic representation.

A small, focused, staff-dominated body has a clear value in relation to executive control. It is not so appropriate for an organisation which is intended to play a wider, advisory role to government on a range of innovative provision. A model for a rather different administrative body for legal aid than the Legal Aid Board model was provided by the Scottish Royal Commission on Legal Services, rather more radical in its recommendations than its disappointing English counterpart. This argued for a body which would have had the following functions:

> . . . the provision of public information as to legal rights and services . . . developing lay advice and representation at tribunals and training for lay representatives . . . studying and experimenting with the best use of law centres . . . grants to advice centres and law centres, the conduct of research, experimenting with ways to provide services, and the setting of standards . . . administering legal aid . . . developing money management counselling . . . publishing advice on how to leave one's affairs in order.[4]

The Legal Aid Board, established by the Legal Aid Act 1988, has less expansive powers, though these do include anything 'which it considers necessary or desirable to provide or secure the provision of advice, assistance and representation'.[5] A new Community Legal Services Authority should be governed by a fundamental objective:

> . . . to ensure, so far as is possible within existing resources, that all members of society, particularly those disadvantaged by poverty or otherwise, have equal access to justice.

The authority should have supplementary powers along the lines recommended by the Scottish Royal Commission.

The Community Legal Services Authority should have a dual role that is reflected in its organisation. A small executive group should be responsible for the administration of what is now legal aid. The other roles proposed for the CLSA should be the responsibility of a wider board that would include representatives of the regional legal services committees. The smaller executive group would then be accountable to the board with its necessarily wider remit.

The community legal service should retain the area structure of the

Legal Aid Board but the operation of regional legal services committees should be different from that envisaged by Lord Mackay. The legal aid budget should not be devolved locally so that each area can make different priorities. This will unavoidably lead to inequalities, inequities and inconsistencies, particularly in the context of a static or declining overall budget. The regional legal services committees should be based much more on the model of the original Manchester committee which was essentially a liaison committee that sought to co-ordinate local legal services developments and inspire new ones. Their aim should be to maximise services within their area, not to advise on rationing entitlement. To do this properly, numbers on the committee should be expanded from the very small groups envisaged by Lord Mackay. Expenses should be paid for attendance and an annual conference held of all committees to compare developments and inspire new ones. The chairs of the committees should be members of the governing body of the service at a national level, as has been proposed by the Legal Aid Board.

Improving the image

Legal aid gets a bad press, as has already been remarked (p60). Much of this is unjustified. Irrespective of any reform of organisational arrangements, attention must be given to present the successes of legal aid more to the public. At the moment, the Board and ministers are continually on the defensive in relation to horror stories about allegedly outrageous grants of legal aid. The Board, irrespective of whether it is transmuted into a new Community Legal Services Authority, needs to develop a better media image of legal aid. The Lord Chancellor should actively promote policies designed to improve legal aid's image.

A simple and desirable way of better explaining the work of legal aid would be to produce an annual profile of all, or a representative sample, of legal aid clients. This has been done regularly by a number of legal aid commissions in Australia and what it reveals is how poor and needy are the majority of both criminal and civil assisted persons. This would provide some support for the allegations of abuse that will unavoidably surface from time to time. The Legal Aid Board or new Authority should take a share of the credit for the cases that it funds: its annual report should discuss them and it might consider participating in press promotion of successes with the practitioners and clients concerned. This would be an important part of forming a better sense of partnership between the Board and legal aid practitioners, a relationship which is currently dominated by a sense of confrontation.

The Board/new Authority could also participate more and more openly in discussion of the civil and criminal justice systems as an entirety. It should seek to maximise the experience of its best practitioners. Thus, the Board or its successor should implement such initiatives as:

— devoting a section of its annual report to recommendations for other 'stakeholders' in the justice system;
— encouraging legal aid practitioners to feed back to it proposals that would facilitate an integrated approach. The Board might encourage groups of specialists to meet: it might also want to start the tradition of an annual conference of legal aid practitioners, part of which could be devoted to consideration of specific areas of practice with the proposal of relevant reform of law and procedure as one of the goals.

Establishing a window into the justice system

In many other jurisdictions, there has been more debate than in this country about how services should be delivered. In particular, countries which have given more attention to social welfare law have tended also to make more use of salaried services, employed both in law centres or their equivalents and directly by the funding body. In some jurisdictions that had earlier followed the original UK example, such as Ontario which first established a judicare system in the 1950s, salaried lawyers were grafted onto the existing service. Ever since, debate has raged over the respective merits of the salaried or 'judicare' services. On cost, evidence from Canada appears to be reasonably conclusive: salaried services tend to be cheaper.[6]

There is an increasing interest in salaried services in England and Wales from a number of quarters. A number of press stories have claimed to document ministerial interest, particularly in relation to public defenders.[7] From another perspective, researchers have been tempted by versions of the same idea. For example, the most thorough recent academic research on criminal private practitioners concluded that the most important difference between good and bad firms was:

> . . . ultimately one of values rather than organisation . . . an important missing ingredient both in current debates over legal aid remuneration

and in potential reforms based, like franchising, on management and quality control measures . . . [8]

The researchers argued:

> There is a case for considering the development of alternative structures for criminal defence work, although not in the form of a monopoly public defence system on American lines or paralleling the Crown Prosecution Service . . . [9]

They floated the idea of whether 'the model of autonomous community law centres', to be known as 'community legal defence centres', could be developed to 'operate alongside and in partnership (rather than in competition with private criminal law practices holding legal aid franchises).'[10] These would have a number of additional roles to those of private practice, including:

> . . . wider responsibilities for community legal education on civil liberties and for addressing general issues of civil rights, such as those surrounding local policing policies and practices.

These arguments raise important issues. First, the researchers are undoubtedly right about their stress on values. These are untested by existing conditions for franchises. Second, there is a powerful case against public defenders, particularly in a country where a Conservative government, initially elected on a strong law and order ticket, grossly underfunded its prosecution service until compelled to put in additional resources. A national defender system is likely to be much less politically desirable. Third, there are positive reasons for retaining properly certified private practitioners in this area, as in others such as personal injury, where that is the current expertise. How many specialists would transfer to a new organisation is unclear. There may also be an issue of culture: the best criminal lawyers might flourish better outside of the corporate ethos of salaried provision. Fourth, there may be, however, a need for community education and involvement on civil rights issues. Where this is the case, there could be some experimentation with the model.

There is another argument other than relative cost for the deployment of a salaried element in provision: that it gives the funder a direct insight into the workings of the justice system. This aids the formation of policy. In Scotland, the Crime and Punishment (Scotland) Act 1997 contains a number of provisions relating to criminal legal aid practice. Its most contentious provision is a power to establish a pilot public defender scheme. After strong opposition from the Law Society of Scotland, this was watered down to a very limited

experiment with an automatic 'sunset' clause so that the public
defenders may only be employed for a defined period of time. The
Scottish Legal Aid Board is ready to proceed with this pilot and has
now been authorised to do so. Its result should provide an indication
of the worth of a directly salaried provision, not as an alternative to
private practice but a complement. It may be that, if a suitable group
of practitioners can be developed which is supportive of the Board/
Community Legal Services Authority, direct provision of this kind
would add little new information. However, it represents a possibility
which other jurisdictions have certainly found valuable. A similar
experiment could be established in England and Wales.

The next chapter discusses the range of services which might be
provided by a new Community Legal Services Authority.

REFERENCES

1 Public Law No 104–134 Omnibus continuing resolution Sec. 503(14) and
(15).
2 LAG, 1992.
3 Ibid, Chapter 10.
4 Royal Commission on Legal Services in Scotland *Report* Cmnd 7846
(HMSO, 1980), Volume 1, para 2.10.
5 Legal Aid Act 1988 s4.
6 For example, P L Brantingham *The Burnaby British Columbia Experiment Public Defender Project: an evaluation* (Department of Justice,
Canada, 1981) and Canadian Bar Association *Legal Aid Delivery
Models: a discussion paper* (1987).
7 See, eg, 'Ministers Study plan for Public Defenders' *Times* 7 July 1997
and 'US style of legal aid is planned for Britain' *Daily Telegraph* 21 June
1997, implying a certain consistency in relation to ministerial briefing.
8 M McConville, J Hodgson, L Bridges, A Pavlovic *Standing Accused: the
organisation and practices of criminal defence lawyers in Britain*
(Clarendon Press, 1994), p294.
9 Ibid, p296.
10 Ibid.

CHAPTER 7

A community legal service: towards a new partnership

The key to success will be to promote a partnership between the voluntary sector, the legal profession, and the Legal Aid Board.
New Labour *Because Britain Deserves Better* (1997 Manifesto), p35.

The history of legal aid has been, as indicated, more about competition than partnership. However, the development of a community legal service offers the opportunity of refashioning delivery of services in a new, broader and more co-operative model. This chapter considers the various elements of service to be provided, beginning with delivery and then dealing with eligibility and the issue of quality. The need to bring down the unit price of cases within a predetermined budget is made the more urgent because not only must existing expenditure be contained but extensions of scope and eligibility are required to make the legal aid scheme acceptably broad. Demands for these extensions cannot simply be put off on the basis that resources are not available. To obtain the kind of public support that is necessary to maintain legal aid expenditure, some broadening of access to it is required. Otherwise, public opinion will increasingly see it as marginal to their interests, going to criminal defendants and a small range of civil litigants.

Social welfare law and tribunals

A Strategy for Justice advanced the argument that there was a particular lack of provision in the fields of social welfare law: housing, immigration, employment, debt/consumer and welfare benefits. Lord Mackay accepted this argument in his green paper, which stated boldly:

The existing scheme does not deliver legal services in areas where there is a clear need for greater help . . . in civil cases . . . lawyers have tended to concentrate on personal injury and divorce work. By contrast, although lawyers do provide help with other legal problems, they do not do so to anything like the same extent. This is particularly the case with what are usually referred to as social welfare problems . . . [1]

The green paper pointed out the disparity of provision between the CAB service where social welfare cases accounted for 70 per cent of all cases and legal aid where they received a mere £45m out of the 1993/94 legal aid budget of £1.2bn. Furthermore, it argued:

Tribunal hearings are not all simple enough for individual applicants to manage unaided. In 1989 a report to the Lord Chancellor concluded that the presence of a representative significantly and independently increases the probability that appellants and applicants will succeed with their case at a tribunal hearing . . . The fact that the advice sector provides such assistance to good effect suggests that there is a gap in the present legal aid system.[2]

These findings have been somewhat forgotten in the aftermath of the subsequent white paper, which did not pursue this line of argument. However, they remain true. More provision needs to be made for assistance and representation before tribunals and in social welfare law cases. They remain continuing priorities: current legal aid provision cannot be accepted as satisfactory.

The issue of representation before tribunals needs to be addressed. The evidence of research commissioned by the Lord Chancellor's Department was clear:[2A] representation by a specialist, not necessarily a lawyer, significantly increased chances of success. Recommendations for the provision of such representation have been made consistently over the last 30 years. The Royal Commission on Legal Services recommended that legal aid should be available for the following situations before tribunals:

- significant points of law;
- 'where evidence is likely to be so complex or specialised that the average layman could reasonably wish for expert help in assembling and evaluating the evidence and in its testing or interpretation';
- test cases;
- 'where the deprivation of liberty or the ability of an individual to follow his occupation is at stake';
- when the amount at stake, though low, is significant to the applicant;

- when suitable lay representation is not available;
- 'when the special circumstances of the individual make legal presentation desirable or when hardship might follow if it was withheld'.[3]

The argument of the Royal Commission as to basic need remains. It identified a list of situations where assistance is required. There is an obvious link between a number of these as they relate to tribunals and LAG's historical approach of identifying essential legal services. However much resources may be in issue, the needs of people must be recognised where they have cases, the results of which are important to them and which are to be determined by tribunals. These have developed significantly from the original idea espoused by the Franks Committee that they could be open to ordinary people as litigants-in-person without prejudice to their likelihood of success. The LCD research has comprehensively exploded that myth. The need for representation in appropriate circumstances must be retained as a continuing one.

The issue of finance is, however, important. In industrial tribunals, there has been the development of lawyers and paralegals working on a contingency fee basis in a way that would be prohibited in court litigation. This does allow an extension of representation but it opens up possibilities of abuse. There should be consideration of the appropriateness of contingency fees which take a percentage of awards for unfair dismissal; there should certainly be the same level of protection as exists in relation to conditional fees in the courts in relation, for example, to maximum charges being no more than a specified percentage of the damages. It may be that there are new sources of funding that could be developed. Contingency fees might be better dealt with collectively under a contingency fee fund which pooled awards and established predetermined levels of payment in successful cases to approved practitioners. Alternatively, awards of costs could be introduced from employers who were found to have, for example, unfairly dismissed an employee. This might be argued to be unbalanced if the reverse were not true and the employee liable if his/her case was lost. However, it could be justified by reference to the public policy benefit of deterring other employers from acting unlawfully.

The areas of social welfare law, particularly those such as immigration, housing and welfare benefits, are distinguished by the extent to which a practitioner must know both administrative practice as well as law. This makes them particularly susceptible to paralegals and lay advisers who can develop a high degree of specialism and expertise. A note of caution, however, has to be added: the characteristics of the different areas vary. Welfare benefits and immigration work are more self-contained than are, say, employment and housing. In these latter areas, basic principles of law, relating to contract or tort, can frequently become unexpectedly relevant. The result is twofold. First, lay advisers or paralegals work best in an environment where there is easy access to lawyers, at best because they work together as in a law centre or agency with a resource lawyer or in a national agency like the Child Poverty Action Group's Citizens Rights Office. Second, it can be dangerous to attempt the kind of separation between legal advice and representation for which the 1986 Efficiency Scrutiny argued.

The role of law centres in creating the agenda for change in relation to legal services for the poor has been, after the genuine challenge mounted in the 1970s, regrettably minimal. The centres have continued to have an influence in terms of cases undertaken and issues promoted, as Chapter 2 indicates, but they have been less influential in terms of the development of forms of legal service, certainly at the local level of community at which they have argued is where they should best be judged.[4] However, the logic of shifting advice to the not-for-profit sector is that representation should follow, particularly in specialist social welfare law areas such as housing. This will require the employment of more specialists, among whom will be more lawyers. A *de facto* law centre sector may, therefore, re-emerge, consisting of some law centres that wish to engage in high volume casework and advice agencies that increasingly take lawyers on board to help with advice and representation. The existing investment in infrastructure of premises and staff means that there would be some logic in placing specialist units within existing agencies, where these exist in convenient locations, rather than developing new ones. The desired model of provision should be a mixed delivery model where, for example, housing services can be provided by the voluntary sector and private practice provided that both can meet a common level of quality. The regional legal services committee will have the role of ensuring an acceptable level of provision over the country.

The growth of commercial paralegal representation in these fields raises issues about standards that need to be addressed. This has been recognised in the case of immigration where the Home Office has become irked by paralegals whom it regards as practicising unethically. Regulation in this field will be difficult but some form of accreditation should be developed, initially perhaps on a voluntary basis. This is better done under the auspices of the Lord Chancellor's Department and within the context of legal services than by the Home Office which, as a party to immigration cases, cannot help but face a conflict of interest.

Ironically in terms of their community-centred ideology, law centres' major influence on the agenda for publicly funded legal services may, in fact, prove to be the development of specialist legal agencies. Together with the longer-established national pressure groups, a distinct sectoral interest is developing in terms of national pressure groups also doubling as centres of legal excellence in their field, a model established for over 20 years by bodies such as Liberty and the Child Poverty Action Group (CPAG). With similar organisations like MIND, these have established the value of a central unit with a mandate to foster developments both in the law and in provision within their fields by way of a mix, different for different organisations, of training, publications, advice, casework and support.

The success of specialist legal organisations concentrating on single issues has been proved internationally. For example, Ontario's specialty clinics have a deservedly good reputation.[5] So too do bodies like the Public Interest Advocacy Centre in Sydney. The national resource centres in the United States have also proved highly effective. This is, therefore, a model that works. In the process of better planning of provision, the success of this model should be remembered and the specialist centres of excellence, with a brief to improve provision nationally by such mechanisms as the provision of training and information, should be established. The current trend towards seeing the planning of legal services as best managed on a regional basis may have the disadvantage that the value of such national units is missed. The Community Legal Services Authority (CLSA) should at least consider a national plan of provision which includes specialist centres for each major area of work. For some, this need not require much, if any, additional finance. Specialist units already exist, for example in welfare benefits (at CPAG) and housing (Shelter). The job of the CLSA would be to provide co-ordination and support.

Eligibility and contributions

A further area where current provision is unsatisfactory is in relation to financial eligibility, both as to the limits of free and contributory provision as well as the level of contributions. Eligibility has dropped to unacceptable levels since 1979. Current levels of contribution are not acceptable. These can be demonstrated by their effect on those caught in the poverty trap: for both families and single people, the impact of legal aid contributions can produce a situation where any additional income has a negative impact. This is the consequence of a wider range of policies than legal aid but the high rate of contributions adds to the problems (see TABLE 8).

TABLE 8: REDUCTION IN INCOME OF PEOPLE ON LOW INCOMES, LIABLE TO TAX AND IN RECEIPT OF LEGAL AID[6]		
Source of deduction	*Family with taxable income but still in receipt of family credit: deduction in pence per pound of income*	*Single person with taxable income: deduction in pence per pound of additional income*
Income tax	20	20
National insurance	10	10
Family credit	49	n/a
Housing benefit	14	45.5
Council tax	4	14
Net income before legal aid	3	10.5
Legal aid deduction	33	33
Net income after legal aid	−30	−22.5

As a matter of policy, this result is ridiculous. At the very least, it makes the case that the percentage taken of income above the lower threshold should be reduced from a third to the quarter that existed before Lord Mackay raised it.

The way forward on eligibility and contributions is to formulate minimum standards that are to be implemented immediately and goals to which eligibility should advance, as funds become available. It is not clear what such reforms would cost but the total bill is likely to be relatively small because many contributions are, in fact, returned because the case is successful and costs are recovered from the other side. A proper calculation should be undertaken from the Legal Aid Board's records. If the costs are deemed too high for reform in relation to all cases, then it may be that some types of case should be prioritised – either those which are considered desirable or cheap – as a first step. The package of reform should be as follows:

- eligibility for free legal aid should be raised immediately so that all those in receipt of family credit, jobseekers' allowance and disability working allowance are entitled without payment of a contribution. Any other result is illogical since the state is creating a classic poverty trap by giving with one hand and taking away with the other;
- an element of contributory legal advice should be returned to the legal advice scheme;
- the ultimate goal for the level of free eligibility for legal advice should be 50 per cent above income support levels. This was the recommendation of the Legal Aid Advisory Committee in the 1970s;[7]
- the ultimate goal for the upper limit should be something like 150 per cent above income support levels;
- there should be a flexible upper limit that operated on a discretionary basis for expensive and desirable cases;
- the amount of contributions should be limited to payment for one year at 25 per cent of the difference between the upper and lower limits, as originally implemented: the percentage of that contribution should reduce from the current one-third to the original one-quarter and eventually down to one-fifth;
- ultimately, the provision of some legal services, defined as being essential, should be without a test of means, eg, those taken to protect against violence, or to protect one's livelihood, home or freedom.

Quality

The Legal Aid Board has been concerned to assure the quality of the work of legal aid practitioners from the moment that it took over responsibility for administering legal aid from the Law Society. Its main approach has been based on 'transaction criteria' (see p27). It is currently exploring, through consultants, other methods, such as measures relating to outcomes. The level of quality expected has been clearly stated to be that 'threshold competence', based on the manufacturing notion of 'fitness for purpose'.[8]

The whole approach to quality needs to be reconsidered, even the level to be attained is much more problematic than has been made out either by the Board or its consultants.

What, for example, do excellent legal aid practitioners omit from the conduct of a criminal trial for murder if they wish to hit the lower standard of 'threshold competence'? Surely, the whole idea of a profession is to carry out work to a professional quality, ie, to the level of best practice. The two research reports for the National Association of CABx show a better way (see p28). These were designed directly to assess against pre-stated standards and in pre-stated categories the quality of work undertaken. Thus, they made a direct judgment of quality rather than the implied judgment possible from indirect methods.

As a practical matter, the transaction criteria approach is falling into disrepute among the better practitioners, first, because of its methodological flaw in only examining procedures and, secondly, because of the practical limitation in its execution which leads to selection of a very small number of files which assessors consider in making an assessment. It is time to move beyond this quality assurance technique, which may well have been justified as an trailblazing early approach to the introduction of quality assurance, to the assertion of objective standards of best practice. The setting of these need require little public money, if any. Representative bodies such as the Law Society should devise them, as the Society has for aspects of criminal work. Legal aid practitioners will be expected to maintain their files in a way that indicates that they meet best practice guidelines. Instead of the attempt at universal approach to monitoring (which has been appropriate for the first phase of implementing franchising), a small proportion of practitioners, with some taken at random and others selected because of complaints, should be the subject of a more exhaustive examination. It may be that the representative bodies might even see the advantage, particularly acute for a professional self-regulatory organisation like the Law Society or Bar Council, in establishing their own control over standards.

Advice: general

England and Wales has a unique infrastructure of agencies, deploying both paid and volunteer advisers, that already provides a considerable volume of advice. This advice sector has argued for a statutory duty on local authorities to provide adequate advice provision and the National Consumer Council has put forward standards in terms of advisers per head of population.[9] In the current climate of financial stringency, the imposition of such a duty might be somewhat controversial. It should perhaps be regarded as a long-term aim. In the meantime, and in the spirit of partnership, the government should recommend local authorities to review provision in their areas for generalist advice of a diagnostic nature. Councils should satisfy themselves that adequate provision is available. Provision of such advice needs to be adapted to local circumstances, making sense of local determination of appropriate services.

The advice sector is increasingly focused where need is most immediate: among the poor. The three largest categories of enquiry to citizens advice bureaux relate to social security, debt and housing. Consumer cases, once the largest category, are now the sixth in volume. The changes to society over recent years (see p7) indicate that this is a response to the need for prioritisation forced on hard-pressed agencies and the local authorities which fund them. However, if the CAB experience is common to the advice sector as whole, then there is a widening group of people with incomes above the poorest deprived of accessible sources of advice. Many will be unable to afford to obtain it elsewhere.

In consequence, government needs to consider whether funds should be available to meet this national need for which local funding is unlikely. The CAB service has experimented with a taped telephone answering service but found, as have others,[10] that this is too insensitive to callers' needs. A number of advice agencies are experimenting with staffed telephone advice provision. This should be encouraged. One way of doing this might be to supplement advice provided through locally funded advice agencies and bureaux by nationally funded services of the kind that could be delivered by phone. Accordingly, there should be an experiment to provide a basic advice service by telephone to callers, ideally on a free basis. Problems of quality assurance in such a service would have to be considered with care: telephone advice is difficult to monitor and control. However, it might be possible to establish such a scheme with commercial sponsorship that allowed a core of experienced advisers to be seconded to staff it. Lottery funding would be an ideal source of funding for such initiatives which would complement greater provision of information (see p91).

In *A Strategy for Justice*, LAG argued that responsibility for the funding of advice should be transferred from the Department of Trade and Industry to the Lord Chancellor's Department. This would encourage the provision of a community legal service that integrated advice and representation. A disadvantage, particularly in an age of fiscal restraint, is that the Lord Chancellor's Department would then have tremendous power over advice agencies, particularly the CABx with their strong national association, because it would control both legal aid and central government grant funding to their national bodies. On balance, the advantages probably outweigh the disadvantages.

Advice: legal

Lord Mackay's green paper identified three elements in the provision of legal services:

(i) initial fact gathering and problem diagnosis covering simply the initial attempt to identify the nature of the application for help;
(ii) basic advice and assistance;
(iii) more detailed problem resolution including court proceedings, representation, alternative dispute resolution.[11]

This assumes that all 'basic advice and assistance' is a common commodity and can be safely placed within the same category. This is wrong. Research on the level of CAB advice suggests that lawyers and lay advice workers may tend to work to different definitions of the nature of advice (see p28). Much advice work may overlap, particularly when given by full-time lay advisers or specialists where their advice, particularly in areas such as social security, employment or immigration law, may be as good, if not better than, many lawyers. However, lawyers are likely to operate at a higher level of advice-giving than that which can reasonably be expected from, say, most of the volunteers that form the backbone of the CAB service. This issue needs the research that it should now receive (see p42). It is possible that the assumption of a difference is not true. After all, the standard of advice and representation provided by lawyers has not gone uncriticised in a recent study of their work in crime.[12] If, however, the difference between general and specialist legal advice is substantiated then each should be funded under different categories. Legal aid money should not be diverted to general advice on the assumption that this is the same as 'legal' advice. To do so would entail a lessening of standards.

The advice sector contains an increasing number both of lawyers and specialists. Advice agencies are already very different, even within an apparently unitary movement like the CAB service. However, the potential availability of legal aid funding for agencies doing 'legal' work will unavoidably draw those agencies more towards a law centre model. A tendency can be predicted for agencies to expand legal advice work to legal representation and to employ lawyers to provide the necessary specialist expertise. The development of a group of agencies within the voluntary sector which can provide a full legal service would be a desirable addition to an area of provision where law centres themselves have stalled in their development. The expansion of existing agencies might represent better value for money than the establishment of completely new organisations.

Legal advice does not have to be provided by the usual model of personal interview. There should be deliberate experiment with, and evaluation of, other ways of providing it. Both the legal aid green paper and Lord Woolf's report on civil justice revealed an interest in the potential of interactive video to undertake this function, at least for some clients with some problems. The effectiveness of such developments in the United States should be monitored with care. In addition, the potential for lawyers, operating on a commercial basis, to offer what have been described as 'unbundled legal services' should be encouraged: this approach encourages lawyers to divide cases into their constituent parts and to offer clients a menu of options over the extent of the assistance provided and paid for.[13]

Representation

The Lord Chancellor has a general responsibility to ensure that adequate legal representation is available to all who need it. This was reflected in the commitment of the Courts and Legal Services Act 1990 which stated as one of its 'general objectives':

> ... the development of legal services in England and Wales (and in particular the development of advocacy, litigation, conveyancing and probate services) by making provision for new or better ways of providing such services and a wider choice of persons providing them, while maintaining the proper and efficient administration of justice.[14]

In relation to the poor and disadvantaged, this duty can be extended to incorporate the objective of providing equal access to justice. This does not require, and should not be limited to, the provision of state-funded representation by way of legal aid or other public funding. The duty on the Lord Chancellor should be to ensure that there is adequate representation of interests for which it is required. Nor does representation need to take the form of individual representation by individual lawyers. Representation could be by a body that takes a corporate or interest group role, eg, the Equal

Opportunities Commission providing representation for women faced with dismissal in discriminatory circumstances. The important point is that the Lord Chancellor's Department commits itself to drawing up a coherent strategy for the provision of representation, however provided, for all the kinds of case where it is deemed essential.

Lord Irvine has launched a review of whether the range of representative actions taken by consumer bodies could be extended. It may well be that this is, in any event, required by European Community legislation. Whatever the origin of this enquiry, it would be desirable for representative actions to be extended. However, further consideration is required to examine what assistance might be given in relation to costs in these and a broader range of public interest litigation. Some legal aid funds, eg, that in Quebec, allow the subsidy of actions taken by not-for-profit organisations. This would represent one solution but it would be difficult to come to an equitable way of determining means. An alternative, which might prove satisfactory, would be to combine rules allowing a broader range of representative actions with a discretionary power to the judge in such a case to issue an indication at an early stage in the case that, if the issues are broadly as they appear to be, there will be no order for costs on the ground that the case has been taken in the public interest. This procedure is sometimes known by its advocates[15] as a 'pre-emptive costs order'. This would leave the representative body to find its own costs, thus providing some check on profligate use of this procedure; give the possibility of some protection against a costs award in the event of failure; but retain judicial discretion and control.

Individual representation does not necessarily imply representation by lawyers. There are areas, even within criminal or civil court cases, where paralegals could provide representation, eg, in relation to procedural hearings. Lawyers, whether solicitors or barristers, have the advantage of clear ethical codes and dual status as officers of the court: this provides good reason why we should be careful in the extension of rights of audience to paralegals who might not be so well controlled. However, there may well be a range of specific court hearings where paralegal representation would be perfectly adequate. The biggest pressure for reform will come from organised institutions with a considerable interest in extending rights of audience in this way, such as the Crown Prosecution Service. Professional interest should not stand in the way of the liberalisation of audience rights begun by the Courts and Legal Services Act 1990. This legislation should, however, be reviewed to see whether its central mechanism of giving ultimate decision-making to the Lord Chancellor and a small number of senior judges represents a correct balance of power. Where representation is not available for whatever reason, then the Lord Chancellor must consider whether assistance is necessary to help the litigant-in-person (see p93).

Regardless of the development of any salaried component of the service, partnership should become much more emphasised in the development of the franchising of practitioners. The Community Legal Services Authority should be working with practitioners to provide a quality-assured service, the original idea, rather than taking the deviation espoused by the Conservative government: administering compulsory competitive tendering among a limited and diminishing pool of providers. If the main way of maintaining control of the legal aid budget is by way of reduction of the unit cost, then the most draconian versions of franchising are not necessary. From the public's point of view, there would be some advantage in extending franchising so that, eventually, a firm must be franchised in order to claim legal aid. This need not, however, be too rigidly applied so that there should be provision, for example, for a client to use an unfranchised firm if it has acted in another matter or where there might be some reasonable cause.

Innovation

Innovation in provision, in relation both to advice and representation should be encouraged. There have been a number of new ways in which legal services have been funded, giving rise to such organisations as the Legal Services Trust and Law For All which have established law centre-type provision, in part with private finance. The Community Legal Services Authority should establish a special fund to encourage innovation. In addition, the Law Society and Bar Council should consider the establishment of a Law Foundation with funds donated voluntarily by lawyers and their professional bodies or taken from the still significant sums available to solicitors as the result of unaccounted interest on their client accounts. The value of such foundations has been well established, particularly in Canada and Australia, where they provide an invaluable source of non-government funding for innovation. That in New South Wales has, for example, established itself as a world leader over the years, experimenting with interactive video kiosks in the late 1980s and currently exploring what can be provided over the internet.[16]

The objectives of the foundation are contained in its founding legislation and are:

(a) to promote the advancement, improvement and extension of the legal education of members of the community . . .

(b) to conduct and sponsor research into the law, the legal system, law reform and the legal profession . . .

(c) to further law reform;

(d) to collect, assess and disseminate . . . information relating to legal education, the law, the legal system, law reform, the legal profession and legal services;

(e) to encourage, support or sponsor projects aimed at facilitating access to legal information and legal services . . .[17]

The foundation's current activity includes the funding of a Civil Justice Research Centre, a Centre for Legal Education, a Legal Scholarship Support Fund, an experiment with Legal Expenses Insurance, a Legal Information Access Centre, a Communications Law Centre, a Litigation Support Fund and First Class Law, its internet presence. This has given New South Wales, a state where legal aid is not that generously available, an institution which has been for two or more decades a world leader. It is a model which should be examined for this country.

The Lord Chancellor's Department

The next chapter looks at the way in which the Lord Chancellor's Department needs to be refashioned to deal with a reformed community legal service of the kind envisaged.

REFERENCES

1 *Legal Aid – Targeting Need* Cm 2854 (HMSO, 1995), paras 3.7–3.8.

2 Ibid, paras 3.14–3.15.

2A H and Y Genn *The Effectiveness of Representation at Tribunals* (Lord Chancellor's Department, 1989).

3 *Royal Commission on Legal Services Final Report* Cmnd 7648 (HMSO, 1979), paras 15.27–15.29.

4 See, eg, Law Centres Federation *Questions of Value* (1988).

5 See *A Strategy for Justice* (LAG, 1992), p83.

6 Using data from a very helpful table produced by S Wilcox *Replacing housing benefit with housing credit* (Chartered Institute of Housing, 1997).

7 Lord Chancellor's Department *27th Legal Aid Annual Reports [1976–77]* HC 172 (HMSO, 1978), p120.

8 A Sherr, R Moorhead and A Paterson *Lawyers – the quality agenda, volume one* (Legal Aid Board, 1994), pp19–20.

9 NCC *The Fourth Right of Citizenship: a review of local advice centres* (NCC, 1977).

10 In the early 1990s, the Law Institute of Victoria and the Legal Aid Commission of Victoria both experimented with telephone advice. The former used tapes and the latter used advisers; the latter was overwhelmingly more successful.

11 *Legal Aid – Targeting Need* Cm 2854 (HMSO, 1995), para 8.5.

12 M McConville et al *Standing Accused: the organisation and practices of criminal defence lawyers in Britain* (Clarendon Press, 1994).

13 See further F S Mosten 'The unbundling of legal services: increasing legal access' in R Smith (ed) *Shaping the Future: new directions in legal services* (LAG, 1995).

14 See s17(1).

15 Chief among whom has been David Thomas, until recently solicitor at the Child Poverty Action Group.

16 See further T Purcell 'Technology's role in access to legal services and legal information' in R Smith (ed) *Shaping the Future: new directions in legal services* (LAG, 1995).

17 Law Foundation Act 1979 s5.

CHAPTER 8

A new role for the Lord Chancellor's Department: information and education

> ... we need to empower our citizens by ensuring that people know what their legal rights and responsibilities are and are clear about how to assert those rights and enforce the responsibilities of others to them ... the [Lord Chancellor's] Department will be restructured in such as way as to ensure that a dynamic, coherent approach to the delivery of legal services is pursued.
>
> Labour *Access to Justice* (1995), pp3 and 7.

The role of the Lord Chancellor's Department (LCD) needs consideration, particularly if judicial appointment is eventually hived off to a free-standing commission. Clearly, the department will maintain a policy-making role in relation to the justice system and legal services. A new element also needs to be added: explicit responsibility for the provision of information and education on the law and constitution.

There might, in the longer term, be some 'tidying up' of functions within government. In criminal matters, the relationship of the Lord Chancellor's Department and the Home Office has come under scrutiny from penal reformers. Baroness Blackstone has argued:

> Unlike a number of European countries, Britain has no Ministry of Justice in which the courts and the prisons could come under the same government department. As a result, those who make decisions about how offenders are treated and who goes to prison are part of a quite different organisation to those who decide the resources allocated to prisons and other penal institutions and the nature of their regimes.[1]

This would be a very radical relocation of responsibilities, transferring large parts of the Home Office's turf to the LCD. There would be disadvantages to such an arrangement: the LCD would then be responsible for both adjudication and disposal; Lady Blackstone is

85

also conflating the role of the judiciary and that of their sponsoring department. A better and more logical realignment would be to transfer from the Home Office to the LCD all responsibility for the rights of detainees from arrest to conviction, with the responsibility for prosecution resting with a Crown Prosecution Service accountable, as now, to a third department, that of the Attorney-General. Such an arrangement would give the Lord Chancellor responsibility for legislation such as the Police and Criminal Evidence Act 1984.

In civil matters, the next chapter argues for more co-ordination of tribunals and courts. At the moment, many tribunals are funded by the departments concerned with their subject matter, though the Lord Chancellor is responsible for some element of their standards and the Council on Tribunals, responsible to the Lord Chancellor, has, in consequence, an overall monitoring brief. In the longer term, responsibility for tribunals might be grouped together under the Lord Chancellor or his successor minister. In the even longer term, the position of the Lord Chancellor could be reconsidered. Labour's 1992 manifesto proposed that the post in its present form be abolished in favour of a Commons-based ministry. Particularly if judicial appointment is removed to a semi-autonomous commission, there can be little justification for the existing arrangements.

Broadening policy

As argued in Chapter 1, the purpose of legal aid and publicly funded legal services is, in essence, constitutional. They represent policies aimed at social inclusion: attacking the barriers which otherwise mean that the poor and otherwise disadvantaged would be excluded from key parts of our society. Labour's Commission on Social Justice argued as the first of its four core ideas that:

The foundation of a free society is the equal worth of its citizens.[2]

From its principles, the Commission deduced a further four objectives of policy: security, opportunity, democracy and fairness.[3] The need for access to justice rests on this approach to social inclusion.

Acceptance of this goal requires a comprehensive response from government that goes beyond the boundaries of the responsibilities of one department. This is institutionally difficult but should still be attempted. The LCD should be responsible for producing a 'justice audit', which ensures that the totality of provision from substantive law to procedural determination is considered together. Less nebulously, it should assume a general responsibility for the provision of adequate information about the provisions of the law. This would require the department to analyse need in a new and cross-disciplinary way. Such an expanded role will require encouragement, fostering and co-ordination more than resources.

The opportunities, as well as the difficulties, can be illustrated by the example of employment law, the content of which will be un-avoidably jealously guarded by the immediately responsible depart-ment. However, there is a need for a more holistic approach. A justice audit would include:

- examination of the substantive law to consider whether its provisions are sufficiently clear and fair;
- recognition that some notion of the rights and duties associated with employment was a valuable component of the educational process during schooling. The Education Act 1988 requires a curriculum to equip students for adult life. Nevertheless, education on citizenship or elementary legal and constitutional concepts has been haphazard. Examination of this area underlines a more general point: schools need to be encouraged to provide more assistance to their pupils on the legal and constitutional aspects of society. This has a 'civics' component, eg, of understanding how our democracy works, but there also needs to be direct identifica-tion of some of the civil law concepts likely to figure in pupils' adult lives, of which employment is a good example;
- recognition that an increasingly diverse and atomised workforce needs access to basic information on law governing its rights and duties. This could be undertaken by a number of providers, among them the government, the union movement, the advice sector or commercial sources. The information could be provided in a number of different ways. Indeed, it should be undertaken by all of these. There should be a national advice strategy which is committed to ensuring that basic employment advice is avail-able throughout the country. This is discussed further in the next chapter;
- information on employment could increasingly be made available on the internet by a range of providers. If free, this would allow access from libraries or other facilities with open access terminals or, increasingly, from computers in homes;
- reform of industrial tribunal procedures that might include a 'pay-ing in procedure' that rewarded sensible advance payments and penalised major underestimates;

- encouragement of a union engagement. It might be that the TUC
  would be ideally placed to provide an internet information service
  that steered users to the appropriate union for assistance;
- development of collective enforcement techniques. Information is
  not, of course, enough. Legal requirements need mechanisms for
  enforcement. Some types of employment problem are better seen as
  systemic rather than individual and dealt with accordingly. For
  example, employers, particularly in some undertakings, have a
  history of paying less than acceptable ways. There should be a
  statutory minimum wage and the teeth should be replaced in the
  Wages Councils process for ensuring acceptable levels of payment
  in low-wage areas of the economy. The cost of collective enforcement measures should be payable by defaulting employers. The
  existence of the Commission for Racial Equality and the Equal
  Opportunities Commission is the result of recognition that gender
  and race discrimination are regarded as endemic. Consideration
  should be given to increasing the finances that they, or any successor Human Rights Commission, have available for enforcement
  and investigation. The use of such bodies may well be more economic than the deployment of individually funded cases under
  legal aid. To an educational role, therefore, must be added statutory and procedural reform. The process of looking at this area of
  provision needs to proceed further through the need for publicly
  funded advice and legal provision as well as the respective roles of
  tribunals and courts;
- assistance with representation at tribunals and access to adequate
  advice.

The fundamental point is that an effective access to justice policy
needs simultaneously to be broad in its solutions and narrow in its
focus on a particular problem. It cannot be approached satisfactorily
by homing in too tightly on legal aid or any successor at too early a
stage in the process. Yet, this has been the Conservative government's
approach. The implication and intention of the legal aid white paper
is that expenditure on employment law advice will be capped at something like current levels and divided between private practitioner and
advice sector providers who may compete on price. Added to the
negative restriction of tribunal jurisdiction, that amounts to a barren
and negative approach.

The responsibility for this new approach will have to rest, fundamentally with the LCD. Carrying it through demands the acceptance
of such a completely new role that there must be some doubt as to

its capacity to deliver. It will certainly need the assistance of a restructured Legal Aid Board/Community Legal Services Authority. It would lead to a radically different and proactive role for the LCD within government as it chivvied and encouraged departments, like the Department for Education and Employment, towards greater efforts in relation to access to justice.

There are some technical matters on which the Lord Chancellor could take a lead in terms of encouraging more accessible legislation. Together with the law officers, the Lord Chancellor could investigate what might be done to make legislation easier to approach by the legally unqualified. Such a review might also look at innovations that have been explored in other jurisdictions. For example, jurisdictions in Australia now have some experience of 'sunsetting' provisions which require secondary legislation to be reconsidered and renewed on a regular basis.[4] This might be of considerable assistance in preventing areas of secondary legislation from getting out of date.

A new information role

As part of this new facilitative role, the LCD should take a lead in relation to the provision of what in Canada is known as 'public legal education'. Labour's *Access to Justice* argued that:

> Schools, advice centres, libraries and court buildings all have a role to play in providing information and promoting public legal education.[5]

Recognition of the need for better information and education is long-standing and widespread. The Royal Commission on Legal Services considered the issue in two exemplary paragraphs but failed to distil them into a concrete recommendation:

> The rights and duties of the citizen are contained in a large number of legal rules and principles to which Parliament adds in every session. Most of us are unaware of the exact extent of these rights and obligations. Many will fail to appreciate that a problem may be resolved by seeking legal advice or resorting to legal action . . .
>
> We recognise that this problem can never wholly be overcome. It can be reduced by a variety of means, for example by devising a pattern of organisation that is not prohibitively expensive, which is able to inform the citizen of his rights and which can direct him to those who can assist him to obtain the remedies to which he is entitled. Other means include

ensuring that schools provide some knowledge and understanding of the law as part of their regular curricula . . .[6]

The National Consumer Council subsequently argued that the right to information and advice should be regarded as a basic, 'fourth', right of citizenship,[7] supporting the need for information both about substantive law, procedure and legal services:

> In order to make sensible choices, consumers need information – about legal rights and responsibilities; about court procedures; about which lawyer to choose; about legal aid; about solicitors' costs; about what to do if things go wrong.[8]

LAG took up the theme in *A Strategy for Justice*: 'Equal access to justice requires all members of society to be aware of their rights and obligations.'[9] LAG argued that a newly created Legal Services Commission should include within its remit a duty:

> . . . to initiate and carry out educational programmes designed to promote an understanding by the public, or by sections of the public, of their rights, powers, privileges and duties under the law.[10]

The difficulty lies in extending recognition of the need for a new commitment to information and education beyond bland verbal support into effective policies. A real commitment to extend 'legal literacy' would represent a new element within the roles undertaken by the LCD, sharply at odds with its previous orientation which has tended to be primarily towards the legal profession and the judiciary. It would, however, be entirely possible for much to be done with relatively little funding. A full information and education programme would include:

- explicit acknowledgement by relevant government ministries (including the LCD, the Department for Education and Employment and the Department of Trade and Industry as funder of the advice sector) that the empowerment of the citizen by knowledge of the law and the legal system is a political objective of the government as a whole and, thereby, should be translated into departmental objectives;
- a commitment that education in the legal system and constitution should be part of the national curriculum, particularly for older pupils who are within sight of leaving school;
- the funding of voluntary organisations (such as the National Association of CABx, other advice sector agencies and the Citizenship Foundation) in order to foster increased legal literacy, perhaps

by setting targets for legal literacy among the population as one of the aims for grant-aid by the National Lottery;
- incorporation of a remit for the encouragement and co-ordination of legal information within the responsibilities of the Legal Aid Board or any successor authority responsible for community legal services;
- implementation of the recommendations about information for litigants-in-person set out later in this chapter (see p93).

Information and new technology

An important part of the new information role for the LCD would be to encourage the use of new technology. The provision of legal services is heavily information-based. No preliminary discussion of the context for policy in this area would be complete without, as a minimum, recognising the extent of the potential for major change in how information is made available and is expected to be made available within society. We must pay some heed to the reality behind the bland statement that we are in the midst of an information revolution.

We can already begin to see some of the possibilities as they may affect legal services for the poor. Information can be disseminated visually at the point of need, as has been seen in the electronic kiosks developed in some US courts.[11] Use of this technology is now beginning to be deployed in this country, with Bedlington Magistrates' Court in the forefront with an interactive guide to the court and its procedures.[12] The beginnings are also apparent of the potential of the internet to provide legal services. Britain's public libraries are bidding to receive £50m to equip every public library with high-speed access. Developments in video-conferencing and distance learning will encourage a new impetus towards educational uses. Public libraries, which have languished in the spending cuts of the 1980s and 1990s, have the potential for an enormous role in extending internet access to those unable to afford it at home. They already have an extremely long reach into the community. There are just under 5,000 public libraries in the UK which are visited by 60 per cent of the population at some time in the year and by 30 per cent once a fortnight. Interestingly, a higher proportion of women (60 per cent) use public libraries than men (40 per cent), offering some possibility of overcoming the male technological lead.[13]

The libraries must play a major role in opening up the internet because otherwise access will be limited to a relatively small proportion of the population. Worldwide, 75m people have access to the internet, with the number having doubled every year since 1988.[14] The number is, however, growing fast, at a global rate of something between 10 and 15 per cent a month. That is to say the number will potentially double something like every six months if expansion continues at the current rate. At the moment, less than 25 per cent of the UK population have a home computer but the potential development of television/cable/internet services could drive that figure rapidly upwards. Already, there is well informed speculation that the development of electronic information systems will change the nature of legal services. As one influential writer has put it:

> My fundamental claim is that [information technology] will enable and help to bring about a shift in paradigm of legal service, a fundamental change from a service that is substantially advisory in nature today to one which will become one of the many information services in the IT-based information society of the future. In turn, basic aspects of the legal process and the administration of justice will also alter radically.[15]

The precise ownership and direction of the mechanisms of change are crucial. They may help to increase access to justice or they may lock up access within the grip of whichever service provider has been prepared to make the capital outlay to set up the IT provision. On behalf of the poor and underprivileged, this is to demarcate a major battlefield of the next few years. The time to prepare for this is now. Already, we can see other countries developing more effective policies for public access to the internet. Just under half, 45 per cent, of all US public libraries have access to the internet. The Australian government has announced its 'Accessing Australia' initiative to provide on-line services at every public library.[16] In the UK, a comparable programme, put together by the Information for All consortium, failed to succeed in its millennium bid for funds. A national network of access to the internet via public terminals in libraries, as argued for in the Information for All bid should be established, using whatever public funds might be appropriate. There have been various experiments with use of the internet for this sort of purpose. For example, the Court for Maricopa County, covering Phoenix in Arizona, has a website which includes information from its 'Self-service Center' that gives information on such matters as domestic violence, divorce, fee deferral and waiver, and tips on self-representation.[17] Experiment with the use of internet-provided legal services should be encouraged, funded both by public and private, profit-oriented, sources.

Adapting to unrepresented litigants

Whatever realistically is provided for in terms of legal aid, the future is likely to see a growth in the number both of unrepresented litigants/defendants and of those represented only on a 'duty' or cursory basis. As a result, there will be a growing need for assistance to people who will otherwise be in danger of not understanding the processes through which, willingly or not, they are passing. Legal representation is absent in a significant and growing minority of cases, even before the Court of Appeal. A report by Lord Justice Otton provided statistics that showed the number of applications for leave to appeal to the Court of Appeal rose from 1,359 in March 1991 when 19.9 per cent were made by litigants-in-person to 2,518 in March 1995 when 29 per cent were made by litigants-in-person.[18] Mirroring the position in tribunals (see p71), unrepresented litigants have a lower success rate in the courts. The Court of Appeal study showed this effect both in relation to applications for leave to appeal and appeals. The concentration on the higher courts masks the fact that the overwhelming business of the civil courts is undertaken at the lowest level. Almost a third of all civil cases are arbitrations in the county court for which legal aid is not available and representation relatively rare.

Thus, there should be policies for providing the kind of service and assistance that is required by the litigant-in-person. This involves a fundamental reassessment of the court bureaucracy, procedure and presentation because, historically, these have focused on lawyers as their 'clients'. In this context, litigants-in-person have tended to be regarded as somewhat tiresome troublemakers who do not understand the system and take up undue amounts of time. A more litigious society which is increasingly concerned about the cost of legal aid can be predicted to create more litigation without representation. Litigants-in-person will increasingly become the norm and courts have to adapt.

This requires more focus on the individual as a consumer to be serviced with care. A number of policies need to be reconsidered. For example, Lord Mackay's policy was to see through a policy of court closures to save money and, overall, improve facilities. The problem is that access, particularly for those now isolated from court centres by expensive public transport, is diminished. Lord Woolf has cautioned against too uncritical an acceptance of the government's court closure plans and for mobile courts to travel in rural areas.[19] As part of cost-savings measures, 19 courts were closed in 1995/96.[20] A similar number closed the previous year. As a result, though there were

270 county courts in July 1995, there are now only around 230. Numbers are shrinking fast: five closed in 1993; 16 in 1994; eight in 1995 and 13 in 1996.[21] The attitude of the Courts Service is expressed with surprising openness in its annual report:

> As a matter of general policy, the overall aim is to improve services to the public by providing them with better facilities. Before the Lord Chancellor is asked to approve the closure of a court, wide public consultation takes place . . . [22]

It seems, therefore, that the Courts Service somehow identifies the improvement of services with the closure of courts.

A different approach is required, oriented towards the needs of users and potential users. This does not necessarily mean that a full court service needs to be preserved wherever one has historically been provided but it does require consideration of what services should be provided locally. In particular, likely needs will include a capacity for litigants-in-person to issue proceedings and for the hearing of small claims cases and minor trials: these could be provided in non-court premises, eg, those shared with a local social services department. Consideration needs to be given to such measures as allowing cases to be issued through post offices or by visiting Courts Service officials in community centres. The power of video, particularly in interactive form, needs to be considered as a way of helping those unfamiliar with court procedures.

There has been a lively debate about the value of the use of such interactive kiosks in a court context. LAG has been enthusiastic about their development in the United States and reported on their implementation in jurisdictions such as Arizona.[23] However, Richard Susskind, acknowledged guru on IT and the law, has argued that they are a diversion.[24] He objects first that kiosks are situated only in court buildings; that stand-alone kiosks will be replaced by the widespread use of personal computers; and that 'court kiosks of today generally suffer from being too firmly tied to the proprietary technologies of their manufacturers and developers'. These are reasonable enough points. However, they can all be overcome by defining the key to the kiosk idea as simply interactive video aimed at educating the user in court processes. As technology develops, there is no problem in conceiving this as provided both to court and other sites, even through the internet to any user who cares to dial into the system. Courts are actually sensible places for stand-alone access to information on court processes. Video offers the opportunity of graphics and a range of different languages. It is very powerful tool. Kiosks in this sense could, and should, play a vital role in familiarising litigants with what for many will be a new environment. The Courts Service should establish a properly monitored and researched pilot, perhaps best situated in the Royal Courts of Justice where it could be an adjunct to the citizens advice bureau already in operation and provide a way of maximising its resources.

The courts

The next chapter deals briefly with some of the issues relevant to policy in relation to the courts.

REFERENCES

1 T Blackstone *Prisons and Penal Reform* (Chatto Counterblast 11, 1990), p51.
2 See, eg, Commission on Social Justice *Social Justice in a Changing World* (IPPR, 1993), p4.
3 Ibid, p5.
4 See, eg, Access to Justice Advisory Committee *Access to Justice* (Commonwealth of Australia, 1994), Chapter 21.
5 Labour *Access to Justice* (1995), p3.
6 *Royal Commission on Legal Services Final Report* Cmnd 7648 (HMSO, 1979), Vol 1, paras 4.24–5.
7 NCC *The Fourth Right of Citizenship: a review of local advice centres* (NCC, 1977).
8 NCC *Ordinary Justice: legal services and the courts in England and Wales: a consumer view* (HMSO, 1989), p2.
9 LAG, 1992; see p113.
10 Ibid, p152.
11 See, eg, R Smith (ed) *Achieving Civil Justice: appropriate dispute resolution for the 1990s* (LAG, 1996), pp41–42.
12 See V Chapman 'A Glimpse of the Future' February 1997 *Legal Action* 8.
13 *Guardian* 7 January 1997.
14 BT *Why not change the way we work?* (1997).
15 R Susskind *The Future of Law: facing the challenges of information technology* (OUP, 1996).
16 *Guardian* 7 January 1997.
17 http://www.state.az.html.us/sp/shelp2.htm; R Smith (ed) *Achieving Civil Justice* (LAG, 1996), pp38–42.
18 Lord Justice Otton *Litigants in Person in the Royal Courts of Justice* (1995), pp9–10.

19 Lord Woolf *Access to Justice: Final Report* (HMSO, 1996), recommend-
    ation 292.
20 Courts Service *Annual Report 1995/96*, p33.
21 *PQ 98/174* letter from M D Huebner to Keith Hill MP, 7 July 1997.
22 Courts Service *Annual Report 1995/96*, p33.
23 See, eg, *Achieving Civil Justice* (LAG, 1996), Chapter 2.
24 R Susskind *The Future of Law: facing the challenges of information
    technology* (OUP, 1996), pp212–214.

CHAPTER 9

Civil justice: the need for a unified approach

> There is a lack of equality between the powerful, wealthy litigant and the under-resourced litigant.
> Lord Woolf *Access to Justice: Final Report* (HMSO, 1996), para 2.

This chapter sketches out how a comprehensive access to justice policy should be applied to the civil justice system. This is important for two reasons. First, an explicit part of Lord Woolf's project was to raise the profile of civil justice which he felt languished in the shadow of the more evident demands of dealing with crime. In taking this position, he was correct. Second, the mechanism of Lord Woolf's report highlights with precision the problems with the hitherto conventional approach to reform. Lord Woolf firmly identified himself, by the title of his interim and final reports, as operating within the traditions of the access to justice movement. However, though he took his title from a phenomenon of the legal services' movement, Lord Woolf did not seek to develop the kind of integrated approach demanded by the grandfathers of access to justice (see p9). Thus, Lord Woolf's consideration of his perceived problems of cost, complexity and delay was undertaken in a way totally divorced from how these issues might be perceived from a legal services' standpoint. This was understandable in institutional terms. Lord Mackay would, and could, not have surrendered Lord Woolf sovereignty over legal aid as well as civil justice: for this, he had other plans.

The result is a muddle that threatens to limit the potential effectiveness of Lord Woolf's approach. The problems of civil justice are not actually cost, complexity and delay. More precisely, it is *excessive* cost, complexity and delay that needs to be addressed. For example, some cost is almost unavoidable either in terms of court fees 97 or legal services: that is why policy on civil justice must be considered together with that on legal services.

Court fees

Since the early 1990s, Lord Mackay's policy has been to raise court fees so that they meet all court costs, including judicial salaries. He set out his position in a speech to the Consumers' Association:

> Subject to certain specific exemptions, charging the full cost of the service will, I believe, provide incentives that will benefit the working of the civil justice system. If ... we want people to make rational choices between different ways of resolving their difficulties, subsidising the courts but not other methods would be counterproductive and would distort choices. Secondly, I believe that if the cost of the service falls on the parties before the court, rather than the hapless and absent taxpayer, all those involved in litigation, including the judges, will be much more careful to guard against unnecessary steps and costly delays. Charging the full cost also reinforces my strategy for ensuring that services are competitively priced ... [1]

This is the classic case for economic rationalism. The problem with this line of argument is threefold: first, it assumes that it is possible accurately to price each piece of litigation at the market rate; second, it assumes that all litigants have sufficient resources to make rational decisions; third, it assumes that those litigants with overwhelming material resources, such as governments and large businesses, will not abuse their position by taking stances which appear to be irrational, as for example in incurring large expense over small matters, but which are economically rational in terms of their own long-term objectives, eg, taking unsupported libel actions as a form of economic harassment, an accusation that has been made against the Police Federation, as well as McDonalds in the long-running McDonalds trial.

These arguments are, regrettably, all false. The Lord Chancellor's Department is unable to attribute costs within the civil justice system with any accuracy. The Public Accounts Committee complained:

> The total cost of the county court system [was] £206 million in 1995–96. We are astonished that, 23 years after its introduction, the Department still does not know how much of this sum is attributable to the small claims service. [2]

Tellingly, officials from the department 'explained that it would be difficult to arrange for each segment of business to recover its own costs because family law work at the county courts almost certainly would not do so' despite the departmental aim of setting 'court fees to recover the full cost of civil business by 1997–98'.[3] It looks, therefore, as if ignorance has been deliberately maintained to allow cross-subsidy of family work. This alone makes a nonsense of any rationalist argument. Around 30 per cent of all civil cases relate to small claims and over 90 per cent of all county court cases are for the recovery of debt. A large percentage of litigants cannot afford to pay high court fees. Judicial review litigation reduced the attempt to end exemption from fees (see p3) for those on income support.[4] However, advisers report continuing problems with a number of other fees that survived the judicial attack, in particular the new £10 fee for variation of a debt order or to suspend an eviction warrant.

What, then, is to be done about court fees? There needs to be a return to principle, despite the fact that this was rigorously resisted by Lord Irvine in a House of Lords debate in the summer of 1997. It is necessary to begin with the constitutional right of the citizen to have access to justice. Mr Justice Laws was correct in law when he stated in his judgment in the *Witham* case that:

> ... the common law has clearly given special weight to the citizen's right of access to the courts. It has been described as a constitutional right, though the cases do not explain what that means. In this whole argument, nothing to my mind has been shown to displace the proposition that the executive cannot in law abrogate the right of access to justice, unless it is specifically so permitted by Parliament ...

Politically, however, that constitutional right should be protected by Parliament in a way that has not hitherto been evident. This should be borne in mind if we move more towards a written constitution in the aftermath of implementation of the European Convention on Human Rights.

Also relevant at the level of principle is an assertion of the public role of the civil courts. An Australian committee on access to justice presented the argument on this ground and in exactly the same context:

> ... it is not only the parties who benefit from the existence of a court system designed to resolve disputes. It is fundamental to a society governed by the rule of law that disputes be resolved in an orderly and principled manner. In this sense, the community benefits from the effective operation of the court system. There is also a public benefit in the form of legal precedents produced by litigation.[5]

Most litigation settles before hearing in anticipation of the ruling of the court; even more cases are settled before litigation 'in the shadow of the law', without court proceedings but in anticipation of their result. That anticipation is based upon the way that previous cases have been decided. This is of the essence in a common law system whose efficacy depends upon litigation taken by others in a way that a civil law system does not. It follows, as a matter of principle, that the argument that all litigants should bear the full costs of their case because they are the sole persons interested in the result is not logically correct.

Until Lord Mackay's change of policy, the courts had sought to recover the costs of their administration but not those of the judiciary. There is no reason why that balance necessarily needs to be retained. The principle at stake is that, however calculated, court fees should be set at a level which lets poor people have access to the courts. Once fees are higher than merely nominal sums, this will necessarily mean that equity requires a means test of some complexity. Lord Mackay attempted to limit the damage to his plans by reintroducing exemption for those on means-tested benefits but this could still mean that those with incomes just above these levels, which are not generous, might still be precluded from the courts. Mr Witham's action was actually for libel where the court fee for issue of proceedings alone was £500.

On the other hand, for some litigants, the level of court fees is not really a relevant consideration, particularly when compared with the level of lawyers' fees. Thus, a sliding scale of contribution can be created which allows for some types of litigation, such as that in the commercial court, to subsidise others, such as family cases. Lord Irvine has revealed that some £100m out of the £257m raised from court users (excepting the £62m from legal aid) comes from:

> . . . large concerns – either issuing claims on their own behalf or paying to support those taking advantage of legal expenses insurance.[6]

This amount could undoubtedly be raised, though this should be undertaken in a way which protects poor litigants from simply having the costs passed on to them as the defendants of corporate claims for uncontested debt. In any event, it would seem prudent for the Lord Chancellor's Department to have some idea of the actual cost of cases. It is important to recognise that the issue of court fees is, in principle, different from that of legal aid. Fees are the guardians of the gate that gives access to the state's courts: legal aid is concerned with representation within those courts.

Some part of the economic rationalist argument could survive if these principles and practicalities were accommodated. For example, it might be decided that the public interest in litigation could be allocated a percentage figure of the total cost. Clearly, estimates could be made of the entitlement to remission and exemption. Following that, the Courts Service could be set targets for the meeting of expenditure, calculated on the 'Robin Hood' principles set out above. Formerly, court fees were determined by a policy that broadly meant that judicial salaries were met from general taxation and administrative costs from court fees. This brought about a pragmatic balance of interest to which it would be advantageous to return and was a reasonable reflection of the balance of public and private interest. It would, however, be incorrect to make this an immutable principle: that is limited to the requirement of access to the courts for all in society.

The issue of court fees interlinks with legal aid because assisted persons are not liable for them. Legal aid is not, however, available in a range of proceedings such as small claims, debt readjustment or libel cases. Remission from fees should, as a minimum, be subject to the same means tests as legal aid and, in any event, be automatically available in all cases for litigants who are in receipt of any means-tested benefit.

Fast-tracks and multi-tracks

Lord Woolf's answers to the problems of civil justice were based upon his perception that these flowed from too little control by the court of litigation. This encouraged lawyers to meander their way through litigation. Lord Woolf's proposal was for the smallest cases to be siphoned off to the small claims procedure. For cases in the middle range, ie, worth between £3,000 to £10,000, control could be exercised by tight rules governing immutable deadlines and limiting rights to such elements as discovery in a way that allowed cases to be processed more quickly and at cheaper cost. In larger or more difficult cases, the court would manage the case more directly. His proposals have attracted considered support and are moving towards implementation. There have, however, been voices of dissent. Lord Irvine has expressed concern at the potential cost implications. Professor Michael Zander did not understate his own position by beginning a recent lecture:

> I have from the outset been extremely critical of the main thrust of the Woolf Report ... My thesis is that implementation of Woolf will disrupt valuable elements of our traditional system, that the hoped-for

compensating benefits will not materialise and that implementation will actually make things worse rather than better.[7]

In relation to the fast-track proposals, Professor Zander just does not believe that the timetable, intended to be around six months, is real-Istic: 'Canute-like, it defies reality.' If this was to prove to be the case then the essential deal – more limited rights, faster hearing times, cheaper litigation costs – starts to unravel.

Professor Zander's objections are sufficiently cogent to require serious consideration. The fast-track could prove disastrous. On the other hand, for some litigants, it could prove a boon. If implemented as envisaged, it offers the advantage of fixed costs, known in advance, and a fast determination. A choice has to be made. The fast-track could, after all, be placed on the back-burner and a less ambitious scheme introduced of more rigid timetabling. One of the most effective, and most simple, advantages of case management systems in the United States is said to be the introduction of procedures whereby lawyers are always operating to a known timetable with a current deadline in terms of a specific date set by the court.[8] This sort of pragmatic reform should be introduced. A fundamental point made by Professor Zander and other commentators has been the lack of research underpinning Lord Woolf's reforms. This contrasts particularly heavily with the position in the United States where two major studies of procedural reform under the Civil Justice Reform Act have just been published.[9] Implementation of unresearched reform is potentially dangerous and it is absolutely crucial that proper pilots over a reasonable period are established if it is wished to explore the effectiveness of the fast-track idea.

One of the potential advances of the process established by Lord Woolf has been the development of a momentum for change. A manifestation of this which it would be wrong to lose is the work that has been undertaken to provide standard protocols for litigators with different types of case. Whatever occurs in relation to the fast-track, the development of litigation protocols covering the preparation of cases should be encouraged by way of cost penalties if there is noncompliance. In all, therefore, the approach to Lord Woolf should be immediate implementation of pragmatic requirements which manifest the spirit of his approach; the commissioning of full research into the potential effect and cost of his detailed recommendations; consideration of the impact on poorer litigants as a specific class; and implementation if appropriate.

Do we want more litigation?

The Conservative government espoused alternatives to litigation in the form of ADR and mediation as good in themselves because they potentially represented cheaper and quicker justice. For example, the government's white paper on legal aid quoted its green predecessor with approval in terms of setting the aim as being to 'encourage the use and development of alternatives to courts and lawyers for resolving problems and disputes'.[10] On the one hand, ADR is hailed by such as the US expert Professor Carrie Menkel-Meadow as potentially 'transformative' of the civil justice system and as thereby further a citizen-based agenda in the terms of Chapter 3.[11] On the other, the government is expressly adopting ADR because it is following its own agenda of cost control of legal services. LAG's own researches into ADR in the United States suggest that it should be seen as a technique which is alternative to courts rather than to lawyers. Most ADR schemes in the USA welcome legal representation and many deem it to be essential.[12]

The role of alternative dispute resolution is an enormous area which was the subject of *Achieving Civil Justice*.[13] In essence, the position taken in that publication is that there should be maximum experimentation with as many varieties of ADR as possible but that there should not be false hopes of the savings that might thereby accrue to the Courts Service, legal aid or private paying clients. The RAND Corporation's summary of its major research project on this subject in the United States bears out the validity of this feeling:

> Our evaluation provided no strong statistical evidence that the mediation or neutral evaluation programs ... significantly affected time to disposition, litigation costs, or attorney views of fairness or satisfaction with case management ... We conclude that the mediation and neutral evaluation programs as implemented ... are not a panacea for perceived problems of cost and delay, but neither do they appear detrimental.[14]

In these circumstances, cautious piloting is a sensible course and should be continued. There should be particularly careful piloting of mediation in matrimonial cases because it might be extremely difficult to avoid additional costs as mediation is imposed on cases which ultimately continue to resort to the courts.

There may be some cases that, as a matter of policy, should be brought more frequently to court. Two groups present themselves. First, those designed to increase the role of the courts as a check on arbitrary action, where the existing judicial review jurisdiction will be supplemented by that of the European Convention on Human Rights if it is incorporated into domestic law. Secondly, there are cases which represent the assertion of rights by groups within society who otherwise feel victimised or oppressed. An example would be women asserting their rights against rape or violence. Attendant costs need to be planned for and provided. For example, incorporation of the European Human Rights Convention may require the establishment of funds for its enforcement. The Canadian government established a funding mechanism and provided the resources for the Canadian Charter of Rights when it became part of the country's constitution. This provides a precedent and it indicates the need to match rights with the money to enforce them.

In recent years, the High Court has developed its role as a check on the executive through judicial review. This may be tiresome for the government and require some further clarity over the limits of judicial activism but it is, in general principle, desirable. Public bodies should act within their legal powers and citizens should have a remedy when they do not. Accordingly, there should be explicit power on the Legal Aid Board to grant legal aid on a challenge where the public interest was involved: this is a point that has been made earlier (p60). In addition or as an alternative, there should be procedures whereby a judge might certify in advance of the hearing of a case that no costs would be awarded, whatever the result.

Into the future

Seeking broader access to justice requires continuing struggle. As an indication of just one of the areas where our justice system needs longer term analysis and discussion, the final part of this book considers very briefly some of the issues of more fundamental civil justice reform. In doing this, it is worth noting that the procedure and organisation of the civil courts of England and Wales have been the subject of three major investigations in the last decade by a government-appointed review body, the legal professional bodies and a law lord. Furthermore, dissatisfaction with the current state of our civil justice system is an almost universal phenomenon in countries with developed justice systems. The Canadian province of Ontario has just published the final report of its civil justice review.[15] Many US courts have been going through a similar process of reassessment.[16] There may, however, be particular reasons to explain the fact that there have been well over 50 major reviews of the domestic civil court system since it was established in something like its current form in the 1870s. There may be fundamental issues that need to be addressed and which have not yet properly been.

All court systems incline to hierarchy. To some extent this is necessary in terms, for example, of appeal rights. The constitutional role of the courts, however, almost inevitably means that reform is slow and jurisdictions carry distinctions that have long since lost their justification. Reform is made the more difficult by the vested interests of those advanced by the hierarchies that might be challenged. Thus, the distinction between equity and common law persisted long after it was helpful. To this day, its traces remain in the division of the High Court into the Queen's Bench and Chancery Division. Thus, proposals to combine the two divisions have consistently been defeated. LAG has argued that:

> There is no reason in principle for the division between the Chancery and Queen's Bench: the county courts, for instance, deal with most of the spectrum of work now split between Chancery and Queen's Bench Divisions. The only truly specialist work of Chancery is to do with trusts, wills, the administration of estates, revenue and patent law. These cases are small in number and, it appears to us, it is a disproportionate use of resources for a separate Division, with separate judges (generally thought to be of above-average calibre), and a separate administration to be maintained simply to ensure a specialised service in these areas.[17]

This remains the case.

Furthermore and more generally, the power of the oral tradition of advocacy, and the barristers thereby accorded status by it, remains as a powerful restraint on change. A discussion paper issued by the Civil Justice Review noted that:

> The various courts, Divisions of the High Court and special jurisdictions which administer Civil Justice in England and Wales may be regarded as a collection of parts or at best a federation of separate activities. It is doubtful whether the sum of the separate parts is so well suited to meet the sum of the need arising. It therefore has to be asked whether the present degree of fragmentation is sustainable or whether it impedes the overall effectiveness of the system.[18]

The review went on to answer its own question with the resounding answer that it was time for an integrated court structure incorporating both High and county courts. Its resolve was soon broken by concentrated resistance from the Bar and the judges. Lord Woolf's review was the direct result because the Civil Justice Review was obliged to recant and scale down its demand to an integrated system of rules. This was the task that Lord Woolf was subsequently set. It is

inherently illogical because the advantage of integrated rules for an
unintegrated court structure is not immediately obvious.

An example of the anomalies which arise from botched reform is
that the majority of the cases in which writs are issued in the
Queen's Bench Division are actually for 'goods sold and delivered,
work done and materials supplied, professional fees', ie, debt. They
account for 19,439 of the 31,737 cases issued in 1995. Somewhat
staggeringly, 11,414 of these debt cases were for sums less than
£5,000.[19] Most of these cases were, no doubt, settled without court
action but their processing by the High Court rather than the county
court is completely illogical. It represents the power of the banks
and commercial lenders who had the political muscle to resist the
fate of wholesale transfer to the county court that befell personal
injury litigation.

What is more, an integrated approach to civil justice would also
require consideration of the position of tribunals. These are as
important to ordinary people as the courts. For example, in 1994–95,
industrial tribunals decided 21,003 cases with a further 21,645 withdrawn or settled before hearing; tribunals covering social security
matters decided 114,995 cases.[20] That compares with 24,477 cases
disposed of by county court trial and 88,170 by arbitration.[21] In time,
we might, therefore, envisage a unified adjudication system. Distinctions between cases would be made by reference to the level of judge
or arbitrator rather than by separate administration and buildings.

As LAG pointed out in its response to the final report of the Civil
Justice Review, there would be additional advantages to such a system
beyond easier and, therefore, potentially more efficient administration:

> A truly unified civil justice system could perhaps allow the development
> of an encouraged career progression through tribunal adjudication and
> into the courts. This might provide in time a cadre of high-quality judi-
> ciary which can operate as an alternative pool [to the existing one of
> advocates, still primarily barristers]. It would be a pragmatic English
> adaptation of the continental style of professional career judges.[22]

In other words, the drive for a judiciary more representative of
women and ethnic minorities might well be assisted by the deliberate
strategy to see tribunals as part of the adjudication structure and to
use them as a kindergarten for the sorts of people who might otherwise find it hard to progress through the current system. This might
be particularly helpful to women for whom a part-time appointment
as a tribunal chair could be more easily combined with care of

children than a job as a court advocate. Such a recruitment initiative could, of course, be instituted without integrating administration.

A further example of the benefits of an integrated approach to courts and their procedures is provided by consideration of whether there are common standards that should apply to such matters as the transparency of decision-making by adjudicating bodies. The European Union has recently published an 'Action Plan on consumer access to justice and the settlement of consumer disputes in the internal market'. An appendix sets out recommended criteria for out-of-court procedures applicable to consumer disputes. This suggests, among other criteria, that 'all decisions must be reasoned and in writing and must be communicated to the parties as soon as possible'.[23] Such a provision should apply all the more to any court or tribunal. Interestingly, there is no statutory requirement on a county court judge to give reasons at all. The parties may require a written note 'of his decision . . . and of his determination of the proceedings'.[24] The authority for the necessity of giving reasons rests on a two-paragraph law report available only in back numbers of the *Times*.[25] It would seem desirable that domestic courts should meet, as a minimum, the standards which the European Union is proposing for out-of-court consumer disputes. Court procedure should be brought into line with best tribunal practice and litigants given a short summary of findings of law and fact together with the decision and its reasons in addition to any order.

Integration of the courts and tribunal system lies a long way in the future. More immediately, we need the implementation of the kind of policies set out in the rest of this book in order to fashion a reasonable access to justice policy. The next chapter summarises the various proposals that have been made.

REFERENCES

1 Speech, 12 February 1997.
2 Committee of Public Accounts *38th Report: Lord Chancellor's Department and the Court Service: handling small claims in the county courts*, para 2(iv).
3 Lord Woolf *Access to Justice: Final Report* (HMSO, 1996), para 43.
4 *R v Lord Chancellor ex p Witham* (1997) *Times* 13 March, DC.
5 Access to Justice Advisory Committee *Access to Justice: an action plan* (Commonwealth of Australia, 1994), para 16.13.
6 Speech, House of Lords, 14 July 1997.

7 'The Woolf Report: Forward or backwards for the new Lord Chancellor', Chancery Bar Association Spring Lecture, 28 April 1997.

8 For example, interview with Bill McNeill, Employment Law Center, San Francisco, 15 June 1995.

9 Federal Judicial Center *Report to the Judicial Conference Committee on Court Administration and Case Management* (1997) and a series of reports from the RAND Corporation including *An Evaluation of Mediation and Early Neutral Evaluation under the Civil Justice Reform Act* (1996).

10 Lord Chancellor's Department *Striking the Balance* Cm 3305 (HMSO, 1996), p5.

11 See her contributions to R Smith (ed) *Shaping the Future: new developments in legal services* (LAG, 1995) and *Achieving Civil Justice: appropriate dispute resolution for the 1990s* (LAG, 1996).

12 See, eg, R Smith *Achieving Civil Justice* (LAG, 1996), p50.

13 LAG, 1996.

14 See n9, pxxvi.

15 *Civil Justice Review: supplemental and final report* (Ontario Court of Justice and Ministry of the Attorney General, 1996).

16 As manifest in, eg, *2022 Reinventing Justice: Report of the Chief Justice's Commission on the Future of the Courts* (Supreme Judicial Court, Massachusetts, 1992).

17 LAG *Evidence to the Review of the Work of the Chancery Division of the High Court* (1980).

18 Civil Justice Review *General Issues* (Lord Chancellor's Department, 1987), para 54.

19 Lord Chancellor's Department *Judicial Statistics 1995* Cm 3290 (HMSO, 1996), p27.

20 *The Annual Report of the Council of Tribunals for 1994/95* (HMSO, 64, 1995), appendix E.

21 *Judicial Statistics 1995* (HMSO), Chapter 4.

22 LAG *Response to the Report of the Review Body on Civil Justice* (1988), para 12.

23 COM(96), p22.

24 County Courts Act 1984 s80.

25 *Banaskiewicz v Mulholland* (1985) *Times* 19 April.

CHAPTER 10

Summary of recommendations

The Labour government has established a review under Sir Peter Middleton to examine the development of its policy in relation to civil justice and publicly funded legal services. His terms of reference are broad (see p47) and his report will clearly be influential. There is a danger, however, that the work done by the previous administration in working towards a 'hard cap' for legal aid and the introduction of compulsory competitive tendering will overly dominate thinking about the future. This book takes Labour's policies on legal services as set out in its 1995 policy document (and described in Chapter 4) in order to examine how a new direction might be set in the development of policy which was able to promise an extension of access to justice as well as control of expenditure.

The government's basic policy should be to seek to extend legal aid's eligibility and scope within the limited budget that it seeks. This will help supply the public support which legal aid needs. In this process, the most enlightened legal aid practitioners and advisers could prove helpful and a partnership should be forged with them. The major recommendations for reform are set out below by reference to the chapter in which they are made.

Chapter 1
Access to justice: a principled approach

1.1 Access to justice is the constitutional right of each citizen.
1.2 The interests of the citizen should predominate in policies on access to justice and not the interests of the providers of services.
1.3 The goal is not only procedural justice but substantive justice.

1.4 People have need for legal assistance both in relation to civil and criminal law.

1.5 Access to justice requires policies which deploy every possible means towards attaining their goal including reform of substantive law, procedure, education, information and legal services.

1.6 Policies on legal services need to deploy a 'portfolio' approach of a wide range of provision, some publicly funded and some not, some provided by lawyers and some not.

1.7 Programmes of reform must take account of the realistic levels of resources but these should be seen as limiting policies rather than defining them.

1.8 Within civil law, more attention should be given than previously to the particular legal needs of poor people currently excluded from legal aid.

1.9 The full potential of technological advances must be harnessed.

1.10 The constitutional right to be regarded as innocent until proved guilty should be respected as a cardinal principle of criminal law.

Chapter 5
Legal aid: how to live within a budget

5.1 There should be no 'hard cap' to legal aid expenditure, ie, no sum which is pre-identified and then divided contractually among providers.

5.2 A 'soft cap' could be put in place in which legal aid expenditure was retained within predictions by way of accurately predicting average costs per case; the number of cases and their average duration.

5.3 Costs should be controlled within a three-year rolling budget but if an absolute guarantee of no excess spending was required then a power could be retained to hold back payments from one year to the next.

5.4 Legal advice has been identified as a candidate for capping but its expenditure could be managed by pinpoint targeting of cuts, eg, of elements of criminal legal advice (but not all) and the amount payable for certain types of welfare benefit assessment.

5.5 In order to expand services, the unit price of existing provision must be reduced by implementation of a number of policies. Multi-party actions might be funded on a separate basis, involving lower costs for the Legal Aid Board. Other high cost cases should be examined, particularly with reference to the fees of

QCs though this should be done in conjunction with the Crown Prosecution Service. The Board should, if practical, work with practitioners to examine areas where savings might be pinpointed. This process might begin with certain Children Act cases. Franchising should be developed as a way of encouraging higher volume, lower cost providers.

5.6 Consideration should be given to the funding of serious fraud cases in a different way.

5.7 An objective test of merit should be retained for civil legal aid.

5.8 The test of merit does not need to be stiffened though its operation by practitioners should be monitored to detect abuse.

5.9 A public interest criteria should be added to the merits test, for example, where the point at issue is one of statutory construction of powers.

5.10 The operation of conditional fees should be reviewed and their extension treated with caution.

Chapter 6
Community legal services: planning and organisation

6.1 An overall figure for projected expenditure needs to be set and then services allocated from within it. The final plan should be published in the name of the Lord Chancellor operating on advice from the Legal Aid Board. The process should be as public as possible. The Board could be formally required to cost various options in relation to provision. The Lord Chancellor would then announce those which had been approved. Regional legal services committees might be encouraged to put forward bids for special projects for which a fund would be established. The committees might also advise the Board on submissions that it could make on cost and need for services.

6.2 A new Community Legal Services Authority (CLSA) should have a basic remit to ensure, so far as is possible within existing resources, that all members of society, particularly those disadvantaged by poverty or otherwise, have equal access to justice.

6.3 The CLSA/reformed Legal Aid Board should have a small executive group overseeing the management of services and a broader group accountable for its wider remit.

6.4 Regional legal services committees should advise on, and facilitate, the delivery of services within their area. Expenses of their

members should be paid and annual conferences funded to
stimulate developments.

6.5 The CLSA/Legal Aid Board should actively promote a positive
image for legal aid. An annual profile of different types of
clients should be published in its annual report. So too should
details of successfully funded cases.

6.6 The CLSA/Legal Aid Board should devote a section of its annual
report to recommendations for other 'stakeholders' in the
justice system and encourage legal aid practitioners to feed back
to it proposals that would facilitate an integrated approach.

6.7 The CLSA/Legal Aid Board should encourage groups of specialists to meet and consider starting the tradition of an annual
conference of legal aid practitioners.

Chapter 7
A community legal service: towards a new partnership

7.1 Legal aid should provide tribunal representation in appropriate
cases.

7.2 The recommendations of the Royal Commission on Legal
Services should be implemented so that legal aid is ultimately
available in tribunals where there are significant points of law;
'where evidence is likely to be so complex or specialised that the
average layman could reasonably wish for expert help in
assembling and evaluating the evidence and in its testing or
interpretation'; test cases; 'where the deprivation of liberty or
the ability of an individual to follow his occupation is at stake';
when the amount at stake, though low, is significant to the
applicant; when suitable lay representation is not available;
'when the special circumstances of the individual make legal
representation desirable or when hardship might follow if it was
withheld'.

7.3 The protection for litigants funded by conditional fees in courts
with lawyers should apply to tribunals and non-lawyers.

7.4 Consideration should be given to some form of contingency
fund for the funding of employment cases rather than individual
contingency fees.

7.5 The ideal model of provision in social welfare law is a mix of
'law centre' and private practitioner.

7.6 The regulation of paralegal advisers should be the responsibility
of the Lord Chancellor's Department.

7.7 The role of specialist support groups should be considered favourably in any national plan of provision.

7.8 Eligibility for free legal aid should be raised immediately so that all those in receipt of family credit, jobseekers' allowance and disability working allowance are entitled without payment of a contribution.

7.9 An element of contributory legal advice should be returned to the legal advice scheme.

7.10 The ultimate goal for the level of free eligibility for legal advice should be 50 per cent above income support levels.

7.11 The ultimate goal for the upper limit should be something like 150 per cent above income support levels.

7.12 There should be a flexible upper limit that operated on a discretionary basis for expensive and desirable cases.

7.13 The amount of contributions should be limited to payment for one year at 25 per cent of the difference between the upper and lower limits, as originally implemented: the percentage of that contribution should reduce from the current one-third to the original one-quarter and eventually down to one-fifth.

7.14 Ultimately, the provision of some legal services, defined as being essential, should be without a test of means, eg, those taken to protect against violence, or to protect one's livelihood, home or freedom.

7.15 The government should recommend that local authorities review their advice provision.

7.16 The case for central funds for central services, such as a national telephone advice service, should be considered.

7.17 Responsibility for the advice sector should be transferred to the Lord Chancellor's Department.

7.18 Maximum use of advice agencies within the community legal service will be assisted by the funding of lawyers and specialist posts.

7.19 The possibilities of 'unbundled' legal services should be considered and developments in the United States monitored.

7.20 The Lord Chancellor's Department, in planning the availability of representation, should consider the role that could be played by representative bodies, such as the Equal Opportunities Commission.

7.21 Public interest litigation should be encouraged by the development of consumer representatives; ways of protecting a losing party from an award of costs and extension of legal aid (see below).

7.22 The Courts and Legal Services Act 1990 should be reviewed to consider whether the involvement of the senior judiciary is appropriate. The appropriate role for paralegal representation should be considered.

7.23 Franchising should be developed as a quality assurance mechanism but a degree of flexibility can be allowed so that, if it becomes exclusive, there are suitable exceptions.

7.24 Consideration should be given to the establishment of a Law Foundation along the lines of that in New South Wales in order to encourage innovative provision.

7.25 Quality should be measured against objective standards of best practice, ideally set by professional associations for their own members.

7.26 Quality assurance should be obtained by a small number of random and selected checks of files.

Chapter 8
A new role for the Lord Chancellor's Department: information and education

8.1 The Lord Chancellor's Department (LCD) should take responsibility for pre-trial criminal procedure.

8.2 The LCD should conduct 'justice audits' in co-operation with other departments.

8.3 The LCD should assume a lead role in relation to public legal education.

8.4 The LCD should be responsible for overseeing a programme that includes: a commitment that education in the legal system and constitution should be part of the national curriculum, particularly for older pupils who are within sight of leaving school; the funding of voluntary organisations (such as the National Association of CABx, other advice sector agencies and the Citizenship Foundation) in order to foster increased legal literacy, perhaps by setting targets for legal literacy among the population as one of the aims for grant-aid by the National Lottery; incorporation of a remit for the encouragement and co-ordination of legal information within the responsibilities of the Legal Aid Board or any successor authority responsible for a community legal services; implementation of the recommendations about information for litigants-in-person.

8.5 The LCD should encourage experiment with the use of such

mechanisms for providing information as the internet and interactive court videos for unrepresented litigants.

8.6   The impact of the court closure plan should be considered from
the point of view of litigants. Court offices might remain even
where courts themselves are shut.

Chapter 9
Civil justice: the need for a unified approach

9.1   It should be a recognised constitutional principle that the citizen
has a right of access to justice.

9.2   There should be a sliding scale of court fees which allows for
some types of litigation, such as that in the commercial court, to
subsidise others, such as family cases. This would implement a
'Robin Hood' principle of cross-subsidy.

9.3   As a matter of priority, the Lord Chancellor's Department
should identify the actual cost of various types of case.

9.4   Remission from court fees should, as a minimum, be subject to
the same means tests as legal advice and assistance.

9.5   Court procedures should require parties to operate a known
timetable with a current deadline in terms of a specific date set
by the court.

9.6   There should be full and proper piloting of the fast-track before
its national implementation.

9.7   Whatever occurs in relation to the fast-track, the development
of litigation protocols covering the preparation of cases should
be encouraged by way of cost penalties if there is noncompliance.

9.8   There should continue to be cautious piloting of ADR and
mediation. Piloting should be particularly cautious in relation to
mandatory mediation in matrimonial cases in order to avoid
additional costs.

9.9   There should be a general statutory duty on behalf of administrators to give reasons for their decisions if required to do so.
Best tribunal practice in this regard should extend to courts.

9.10 In the longer term, fundamental restructuring of the structure
of courts and tribunals should be borne in mind.

Index

117

118 *Index*